# THE DAILY STUDY BIBLE SERIES
### REVISED EDITION

### THE LETTER TO THE
## HEBREWS

# THE LETTER TO THE
# HEBREWS

### REVISED EDITION

Translated
with an Introduction and Interpretation
by
## WILLIAM  BARCLAY

## THE  WESTMINSTER  PRESS
### PHILADELPHIA

Revised Edition
Copyright © 1976 William Barclay

First published by The Saint Andrew Press
Edinburgh, Scotland

First Edition, March, 1955

Second Edition, April, 1957

Published by The Westminster Press®
Philadelphia, Pennsylvania

PRINTED IN THE UNITED STATES OF AMERICA

*Second Printing, 1977*

To D.A.

FOR ALL HIS MANY KINDNESSES TO ME

AND ESPECIALLY

BECAUSE IT WAS AT HIS REQUEST

THAT I WROTE THIS BOOK

**Library of Congress Cataloging in Publication Data**

Bible. N.T. Hebrews. English. Barclay. 1976.
　　The Letter to the Hebrews.

　　(The Daily study Bible series. — Rev. ed.)
　　1. Bible. N.T. Hebrews — Commentaries.
I. Barclay, William, lecturer in the University of
Glasgow. II. Title. III. Series.
BS2773.B37　1976　　　227'.87'077　　　75-37611
ISBN 0-664-21312-X
ISBN 0-664-24112-3 pbk.

# GENERAL INTRODUCTION

*The Daily Study Bible* series has always had one aim—to convey the results of scholarship to the ordinary reader. A. S. Peake delighted in the saying that he was a "theological middleman", and I would be happy if the same could be said of me in regard to these volumes. And yet the primary aim of the series has never been academic. It could be summed up in the famous words of Richard of Chichester's prayer—to enable men and women "to know Jesus Christ more clearly, to love him more dearly, and to follow him more nearly".

It is all of twenty years since the first volume of *The Daily Study Bible* was published. The series was the brain-child of the late Rev. Andrew McCosh, M.A., S.T.M., the then Secretary and Manager of the Committee on Publications of the Church of Scotland, and of the late Rev. R. G. Macdonald, O.B.E., M.A., D.D., its Convener.

It is a great joy to me to know that all through the years *The Daily Study Bible* has been used at home and abroad, by minister, by missionary, by student and by layman, and that it has been translated into many different languages. Now, after so many printings, it has become necessary to renew the printer's type and the opportunity has been taken to restyle the books, to correct some errors in the text and to remove some references which have become outdated. At the same time, the Biblical quotations within the text have been changed to use the Revised Standard Version, but my own original translation of the New Testament passages has been retained at the beginning of each daily section.

There is one debt which I would be sadly lacking in courtesy if I did not acknowledge. The work of revision and correction has been done entirely by the Rev. James Martin, M.A., B.D., minister of High Carntyne Church, Glasgow. Had it not been for him this task would never have been undertaken, and it is impossible for me to thank him enough for the selfless toil he has put into the revision of these books.

It is my prayer that God may continue to use *The Daily Study Bible* to enable men better to understand His word.

Glasgow  WILLIAM BARCLAY

# CONTENTS

viii CONTENTS

# INTRODUCTION TO THE LETTER TO
# THE HEBREWS

GOD FULFILS HIMSELF IN MANY WAYS

Religion has never been the same thing to all men. "God," as Tennyson said, "fulfils himself in many ways." George Russell said: "There are as many ways of climbing to the stars as there are people to climb." There is a well-known saying which tells us very truly and very beautifully that "God has his own secret stairway into every heart." Broadly speaking, there have been four great conceptions of religion.

(i) To some men it is *inward fellowship with God*. It is a union with Christ so close and so intimate that the Christian can be said to live in Christ and Christ to live in him. That was Paul's conception of religion. To him it was something which mystically united him with God.

(ii) To some religion is what gives a man *a standard for life and a power to reach that standard*. On the whole that is what religion was to James and to Peter. It was something which showed them what life ought to be and which enabled them to attain it.

(iii) To some men religion is *the highest satisfaction of their minds*. Their minds seek and seek until they find that they can rest in God. It was Plato who said that "the unexamined life is the life not worth living." There are some men who must understand or perish. On the whole that is what religion was to John. The first chapter of his gospel is one of the greatest attempts in the world to state religion in a way that really satisfies the mind.

(iv) To some men religion is *access to God*. It is that which removes the barriers and opens the door to his living presence. That is what religion was to the writer of the Letter to the Hebrews. With that idea his mind was dominated. He found in

Christ the one person who could take him into the very presence of God. His whole idea of religion is summed up in the great passage in *Hebrews* 10: 19–23.

> "Therefore, since we have confidence to enter the sanctuary by the blood of Jesus, by the new and living way which he opened for us through the curtain, that is, through his flesh, . . . let us draw near with a true heart in full assurance of faith."

If the writer to the Hebrews had one text it was: "*Let us draw near.*"

### THE DOUBLE BACKGROUND

The writer to the Hebrews had a double background into both of which this idea came. He had a *Greek background.* Ever since the time of Plato, five hundred years before, the Greeks had been haunted by the contrast between the real and the unreal, the seen and the unseen, the temporal and the eternal. It was the Greek idea that somewhere there was a real world of which this was only a shadowy and imperfect copy. Plato had the idea that somewhere there was a world of perfect *forms* or *ideas* or *patterns*, of which everything in this world was an imperfect copy. To take a simple instance, somewhere there was laid up the pattern of a perfect chair of which all the chairs in this world were inadequate copies. Plato said: "The Creator of the world had designed and carried out his work according to an unchangeable and eternal pattern of which the world is but a copy." Philo, who took his ideas from Plato, said: "God knew from the beginning that a fair copy could never come into being apart from a fair pattern; and that none of the objects perceivable by sense could be flawless which was not modelled after an archetype and spiritual idea, and thus, when he prepared to create this visible world, he shaped beforehand the ideal world in order to constitute the corporeal after the incorporeal and godlike pattern." When Cicero was talking of the laws men know and use on earth, he said: "We have no real and life-like likeness of real law and genuine justice; all we enjoy is a shadow and a sketch."

The thinkers of the ancient world all had this idea that somewhere there is a real world of which this one is only a kind of imperfect copy. Here we can only guess and grope; here we can work only with copies and imperfect things. But in the unseen world there are the real and perfect things. When Newman died they erected a statue to him, and on the pedestal of it are the Latin words: *Ab umbris et imaginibus ad veritatem,* "Away from the shadows and the semblances to the truth." If that be so, clearly the great task of this life is to get away from the shadows and the imperfections and to reach *reality.* This is exactly what the writer to the Hebrews claims that Jesus Christ can enable us to do. To the Greek the writer to the Hebrews said: "All your lives you have been trying to get from the shadows to the truth. That is just what Jesus Christ can enable you to do."

### THE HEBREW BACKGROUND

But the writer to the Hebrews also had a *Jewish background.* To the Jew it was always dangerous to come too near to God. "Man," said God to Moses, "shall not see me and live" (*Exodus* 33: 20). It was Jacob's astonished exclamation at Peniel: "I have seen God face to face and yet my life is preserved" (*Genesis* 32: 30). When Manoah realised who his visitor had been, he said in terror to his wife: "We shall surely die, for we have seen God." The great day of Jewish worship was the Day of Atonement. That was the one day of all the year when the High Priest entered the Holy of Holies where the very presence of God was held to dwell. No man ever entered in except the High Priest, and he only on that day. When he did, the law laid it down that he must not linger in the Holy Place for long "lest he put Israel in terror." It was dangerous to enter the presence of God and if a man waited too long he might be struck dead.

In view of this there entered into Jewish thought the idea of a *covenant.* God, in his grace and in a way that was quite unmerited, approached the nation of Israel and offered them a special relationship with himself. But this unique access to

God was conditional on the observance by the people of the law that he gave to them. We can see this relationship being entered into and this law being accepted in the dramatic scene in *Exodus* 24: 3–8.

So then Israel had access to God, *but only if she kept the law.* To break the law was sin, and sin put up a barrier which stopped the way to God. It was to take away that barrier that the system of the Levitical priesthood and sacrifices was constructed. The law was given; man sinned; the barrier was up; the sacrifice was made; and the sacrifice was designed to open the closed way to God. But the experience of life was that this was precisely what sacrifice could not do. It was proof of the ineffectiveness of the whole system that sacrifice had to go on and on and on. It was a losing and ineffective battle to remove the barrier that sin had erected between man and God.

### THE PERFECT PRIEST AND THE PERFECT SACRIFICE

What men needed was a *perfect priest* and a *perfect sacrifice*, someone who was such that he could bring to God a sacrifice which once and for all opened the way of access to him. That, said the writer to the Hebrews, is exactly what Christ did. He is the perfect priest because he is at once perfectly man and perfectly God. In his manhood he can take man to God and in his Godhead he can take God to man. He has no sin. The perfect sacrifice he brings is the sacrifice of himself, a sacrifice so perfect that it never needs to be made again. To the Jew the writer to the Hebrews said: "All your lives you have been looking for the perfect priest who can bring the perfect sacrifice and give you access to God. You have him in Jesus Christ and in him alone."

To the Greek the writer to the Hebrews said: "You are looking for the way from the shadows to reality; you will find it in Jesus Christ." To the Jew the writer to the Hebrews said: "You are looking for that perfect sacrifice which will open the way to God which your sins have closed; you

will find it in Jesus Christ." Jesus was the one person who
gave access to reality and access to God. That is the key-
thought of this letter.

THE RIDDLE OF THE NEW TESTAMENT

So much is clear but when we turn to the other questions
of introduction Hebrews is wrapped in mystery. E. F. Scott
wrote: "The Epistle to the Hebrews is in many respects the
riddle of the New Testament." When it was written, to whom
it was written, and who wrote it are questions at which we
can only guess. The very history of the letter shows how its
mystery it to be treated with a certain reserve and suspicion. It
was a long time before it became an unquestioned New
Testament book. The first list of New Testament books, The
Muratorian Canon, compiled about A.D. 170, does not
mention it at all. The great Alexandrian scholars, Clement
and Origen, knew it and loved it but agreed that its place as
scripture was disputed. Of the great African fathers, Cyprian
never mentions it and Tertullian knows that its place was
disputed. Eusebius, the great Church historian, says that it
ranked among the disputed books. It was not until the time
of Athanasius, in the middle of the fourth century, that
*Hebrews* was definitely accepted as a New Testament book,
and even Luther was not too sure about it. It is strange to
think how long this great book had to wait for full recognition.

WHEN WAS IT WRITTEN?

The only information we have comes from the letter itself.
Clearly it is written for what we might call second generation
Christians (2: 3). The story was transmitted to its recipients
by those who had heard the Lord. The community to whom
it was written were not new to the Christian faith; they
ought to have been mature (5: 12). They must have had a
long history for they are summoned to look back on the
former days (10: 32). They had a great history behind them
and heroic martyr figures on which they ought to look back
for inspiration (13: 7).

The thing that will help us most in dating the letter is its references to persecution. It is clear that at one time their leaders had died for their faith (13: 7). It is clear that they themselves had not yet suffered persecution, for they had not yet resisted to the point of shedding their blood (12: 4). It is also clear that they have had ill-treatment to suffer for they have had to undergo the pillaging of their goods (10: 32–34). And it is clear from the outlook of the letter that there is a risk of persecution about to come. From all that it is safe to say that this letter must have been written between two persecutions, in days when Christians were not actually persecuted, but were none the less unpopular with their fellow-men. Now the first persecution was in the time of Nero in the year A.D. 64; and the next was in the time of Domitian about A.D. 85. Somewhere between these dates this letter was written, more likely nearer to Domitian. If we take the date as A.D. 80 we shall not be far wrong.

TO WHOM WAS IT WRITTEN?

Once again we have to be dependent on such hints as we get from the letter itself. One thing is certain—it cannot have been written to any of the great Churches or the name of the place could not have so completely vanished. Let us set down what we know. The letter was written to a long-established Church (5: 12). It was written to a Church which had at some time in the past suffered persecution (10: 32–34). It was written to a Church which had had great days and great teachers and leaders (13: 7). It was written to a Church which had not been directly founded by the apostles (2: 3). It was written to a Church which had been marked by generosity and liberality (6: 10).

We do have one direct hint. Amongst the closing greetings we find the sentence, as the Revised Standard Version translates it: "Those who come from Italy send you greetings" (13: 24). Taken by itself that phrase could mean either that the letter was written *from* Italy or that it was written *to* Italy, the greater likelihood is that it was written *to* Italy. Suppose I am in

Glasgow and am writing to some place abroad. I would not be likely to say, "All the people from Glasgow greet you." I would be much more likely to say, "All the people in Glasgow greet you." But suppose I am somewhere abroad where there is a little colony of Glaswegians, I might well say, "All the people from Glasgow send you their greetings." So then we may say that the letter was written *to Italy*; and if it was written to Italy it was almost certainly written to Rome.

But quite certainly it was not written to the Church at Rome as a whole. If it had been it would never have lost its title. Furthermore, it gives the unmistakable impression that it was written to a small body of like-minded persons. Moreover, it was obviously written to a scholarly group. From 5: 12 we can see that they had long been under instruction and were preparing themselves to become teachers of the Christian faith. Still further, *Hebrews* demands such a knowledge of the Old Testament that it must always have been a book written by a scholar for scholars.

When we sum it all up, we can say that *Hebrews* is a letter written by a great teacher to a little group or college of Christians in Rome. He was their teacher; at the moment he was separated from them and was afraid that they were drifting away from the faith; and so he wrote this letter to them. It is not so much a letter as a talk. It does not begin like Paul's letters do, although it ends with greetings as a letter does. The writer himself calls it "a word of exhortation."

### BY WHOM WAS IT WRITTEN?

Perhaps the most insoluble problem of all is the problem of its authorship. It was precisely that uncertainty which kept it so long on the fringes of the New Testament. The title in the earliest days was simply, "To the Hebrews." No author's name was given, no one connected it directly with the name of Paul. Clement of Alexandria used to think that Paul might have written it in Hebrew and that Luke translated it, for the style is quite different from that of Paul. Origen made a famous remark, "who wrote the *Letter to the Hebrews* only

God knows for certain." Tertullian thought that Barnabas wrote it. Jerome said the Latin Church did not receive it as Paul's and speaking of the author said, "the writer to the Hebrews whoever he was." Augustine felt the same way about it. Luther declared that Paul could never have written it because the thought was not his. Calvin said that he could not bring himself to think that this letter was a letter of Paul.

At no time in the history of the Church did men ever really think that Paul wrote *Hebrews*. How then did it get attached to his name? It happened very simply. When the New Testament came into its final form there was of course argument about which books were to be included and which were not. To settle it one test was used. Was a book the work of an apostle or at least the work of one who had been in direct contact with the apostles? By this time *Hebrews* was known and loved throughout the Church. Most people felt like Origen that God alone knew who wrote it, but they wanted it. They felt it *must* go into the New Testament and the only way to ensure that was to include it with the thirteen letters of Paul. *Hebrews* won its way into the New Testament on the grounds of its own greatness, but to get in it had to be included with the letters of Paul and come under his name. People knew quite well that it was not Paul's but they included it among his letters because no man knew who wrote it and yet it must go in.

THE AUTHOR OF HEBREWS

Can we guess who the author was? Many candidates have been put forward. We can only glance at three of the many suggestions.

(i) Tertullian thought that Barnabas wrote it. Barnabas was a native of Cyprus, the people of Cyprus were famous for the excellence of the Greek they spoke; and *Hebrews* is written in the best Greek in the New Testament. He was a Levite (*Acts* 4: 36) and of all men in the New Testament he would have had the closest knowledge of the priestly and sacrificial system on which the whole thought of the letter is based. He is called a son of *encouragement*; the Greek word is *paraklēsis*; and *Hebrews* calls itself a word of *paraklēsis* (13: 22). He was one of the few men acceptable to both Jews and Greeks and at home in both worlds of thought. It might be that Barnabas wrote this letter, but if so it is strange that his name should vanish in connection with it.

(ii) Luther was sure that Apollos was the author. Apollos, according to the New Testament mention of him, was a Jew, born at Alexandria, an eloquent man and mighty in the scriptures (*Acts* 18: 24ff.; 1 *Corinthians* 1: 12; 3: 4). The man who wrote this letter knew the scriptures; he was eloquent; and he thought and argued in the way that a cultured Alexandrian would. The man who wrote *Hebrews* was certainly a man like Apollos in thought and in background.

(iii) The most romantic of all conjectures is that of Harnack, the great German scholar. He thought that maybe Aquila and Priscilla wrote it between them. Aquila was a teacher (*Acts* 18: 26). Their house in Rome was a Church in itself (*Romans* 16: 5). Harnack thought that that is why the letter begins with no greetings and why the writer's name has vanished—because the main author of *Hebrews* was a woman and a woman was not allowed to teach.

But when we come to the end of conjecture, we are compelled to say as Origen said seventeen hundred years ago, that only God knows who wrote *Hebrews*. To us the author must remain a voice and nothing more, but we can be thankful to God for the work of this great nameless one who wrote with incomparable skill and beauty about the Jesus who is the way to reality and the way to God.

# HEBREWS

## THE END OF FRAGMENTS

*Hebrews* 1: 1–3

> It was in many parts and in many ways that God spoke to our
> fathers in the prophets in time gone past; but in the end of these
> days he has spoken to us in One who is a Son, a Son whom he
> destined to enter into possession of all things, a Son by whose
> agency he made the universe. He was the very effulgence of God's
> glory; he was the exact expression of God's very essence. He bore
> everything onwards by the word of his power; and after he had
> made purification for the sins of men, he took his royal seat at
> the right hand of the glory in the heights.

THIS is the most sonorous piece of Greek in the whole New
Testament. It is a passage that any classical Greek orator
would have been proud to write. The writer of *Hebrews* has
brought to it every artifice of word and rhythm that the
beautiful and flexible Greek language could provide. In
Greek the two adverbs which we have translated *in many parts*
and *in many ways* are single words, *polumerōs* and *polutropōs*.
*Polu-* in such a combination means *many* and it was a habit
of the great Greek orators, like Demosthenes, the greatest of
them all, to weave such sonorous words into the first
paragraph of a speech. The writer to the Hebrews felt that,
since he was going to speak of the supreme revelation of
God to men, he must clothe his thought in the noblest
language that it was possible to find.

There is something of interest even here. The man who
wrote this letter must have been trained in Greek oratory.
When he became a Christian he did not throw his training
away. *He used the talent he had in the service of Jesus Christ.*
Everyone knows the lovely legend of the acrobatic tumbler
who became a monk. He felt that he had so little to offer.
One day someone saw him go into the chapel and stand
before the statue of the Virgin Mary. He hesitated for a

moment and then began to go through his acrobatic routine. When he had completed his tumbling, he knelt in adoration; and then, says the legend, the statue of the Virgin Mary came to life, stepped down from her pedestal and gently wiped the sweat from the brow of the acrobat who had offered all he had to give. When a man becomes a Christian he is not asked to abandon all the talents he once had; he is asked to use them in the service of Jesus Christ and of his Church.

The basic idea of this letter is that Jesus Christ alone brings to men the full revelation of God and that he alone enables them to enter into his very presence. The writer begins by contrasting Jesus with the prophets who had gone before. He talks about him coming *in the end of these days*. The Jews divided all time into two ages—the present age and the age to come. In between they set The Day of the Lord. The present age was wholly bad; the age to come was to be the golden age of God. The Day of the Lord was to be like the birth-pangs of the new age. So the writer to the Hebrews says, "The old time is passing away; the age of incompleteness is gone; the time of human guessing and groping is at an end; the new age, the age of God, has dawned in Christ." He sees the world and the thought of men enter, as it were, into a new beginning with Christ. In Jesus God has entered humanity, eternity has invaded time, and things can never be the same again.

He contrasts Jesus with the prophets, for they were always believed to be in the secret counsels of God. Long ago Amos had said: "The Lord God does nothing without revealing his secrets to his servants the prophets" (*Amos* 3: 7). Philo had said: "The prophet is the interpreter of the God who speaks within." He had said: "The prophets are interpreters of the God who uses them as instruments to reveal to men that which he wills." In later days this doctrine had been completely mechanized. Athenagoras spoke of God moving the mouths of the prophets as a man might play upon a musical instrument and of the Spirit breathing into them as a flute-player breathes into a flute. Justin Martyr spoke of the divine coming down from heaven and sweeping across the prophets as a plectrum sweeps across a harp or a lute. In the end men came to put it in such a way that the prophets had really no more to do with their message than a musical instrument had to do with the music it played or a pen with the message it wrote. That was over-mechanizing the matter; for even the finest musician is to some extent at the mercy of his instrument and can not produce great music out of a piano in which certain notes are missing or out of tune, and even the finest penman is to some extent at the mercy of his pen. God can not reveal more than men can understand. His revelation comes through the minds and the hearts of men. That is exactly what the writer to the Hebrews saw.

He says that the revelation of God which came through the prophets was *in many parts* (*polumerōs*) and *in many ways* (*polutropōs*). There are two ideas there.

(i) The revelation of the prophets had a variegated grandeur which made it a tremendous thing. From age to age they had spoken, always fitting their message to the age, never letting it be out of date. At the same time, that revelation was *fragmentary* and had to be presented in such a way that the limitations of the time would understand. One of the most interesting things is to see how time and again the prophets are characterized by one idea. For instance, *Amos* is "*a cry for social justice.*" *Isaiah* had grasped the *holiness of God. Hosea,* because of his own bitter home experience, had realized the wonder of *the forgiving love of God.* Each prophet, out of his own experience of life and out of the experience of Israel, had grasped and expressed a *fragment* of the truth of God. None had grasped the whole round orb of truth; but with Jesus it was different. He was not a fragment of the truth; he was the whole truth. In him God displayed not some part of himself but all of himself.

(ii) The prophets used many methods. They used the method of *speech.* When speech failed they used the method of *dramatic action* (Cp. 1 *Kings* 11: 29–32; *Jeremiah* 13: 1–9; 27: 1–7; *Ezekiel* 4: 1–3; 5: 1–4). The prophet had to use human methods to transmit his part of the truth of God.

Again, it was different with Jesus. He revealed God *by being himself*. It was not so much what he said and did that shows us what God is like; it is what he was.

The revelation of the prophets was great and manifold, but it was fragmentary and presented by such methods as they could find to make it effective. The revelation of God in Jesus was complete and was presented in Jesus himself. In a word, the prophets were the *friends* of God; but Jesus was the *Son*. The prophets grasped *part* of the mind of God; but Jesus *was* that mind. It is to be noted that it is no part of the purpose of the writer to the Hebrews to belittle the prophets; it is his aim to establish the supremacy of Jesus Christ. He is not saying that there is a *break* between the Old Testament revelation and that of the New Testament; he is stressing the fact that there is *continuity*, but continuity that ends in *consummation*.

The writer to the Hebrews uses two great pictures to describe what Jesus was. He says that he was the *apaugasma* of God's glory. *Apaugasma* can mean one of two things in Greek. It can mean *effulgence*, the light which shines forth, or it can mean *reflection*, the light which is reflected. Here it probably means *effulgence*. Jesus is the shining of God's glory among men.

He says that he was the *charactēr* of God's very essence. In Greek *charactēr* means two things, first, a *seal*, and, second, the *impression* that the seal leaves on the wax. The impression has the exact form of the seal. So, when the writer to the Hebrews said that Jesus was the *charactēr* of the being of God, he meant that he was the exact image of God. Just as when you look at the impression, you see exactly what the seal which made it is like, so when you look at Jesus you see exactly what God is like.

C. J. Vaughan has pointed out that this passage tells us six great things about Jesus.

(i) The original glory of God belongs to him. Here is a wonderful thought. Jesus is God's glory; therefore, we see with amazing clarity that the glory of God consists not in crushing men and reducing them to abject servitude, but in serving them and loving them and in the end dying for them.

It is not the glory of shattering power but the glory of suffering love.

(ii) The destined empire belongs to Jesus. The New Testament writers never doubted his ultimate triumph. Think of it. They were thinking of a Galilaean carpenter who was crucified as a criminal on a cross on a hill outside the city of Jerusalem. They themselves faced savage persecution and were the humblest of people. As Sir William Watson said of them,

> "So to the wild wolf Hate were sacrificed
> The panting, huddled flock, whose crime was Christ."

And yet they never doubted the eventual victory. They were quite certain that God's love was backed by his power and that in the end the kingdoms of the world would be the kingdoms of the Lord and of his Christ.

(iii) The creative action belongs to Jesus. The early Church held that the Son had been God's agent in creation, that in some way God had originally created the world through him. They were filled with the thought that the One who had created the world would also be the One who redeemed it.

(iv) The sustaining power belongs to Jesus. These early Christians had a tremendous grip of the doctrine of *providence*. They did not think of God as creating the world and then leaving it to itself. Somehow and somewhere they saw a power that was carrying the world and each life on to a destined end. They believed,

> "That nothing walks with aimless feet;
> That not one life shall be destroy'd,
> Or cast as rubbish to the void,
> When God hath made the pile complete."

(v) To Jesus belongs the redemptive work. By his sacrifice he paid the price of sin; by his continual presence he liberates from sin.

(vi) To Jesus belongs the mediatorial exaltation. He has taken his place on the right hand of glory; but the tremendous thought of the writer to the Hebrews is that he is there, not as our judge but as one who makes intercession for us so that, when we enter into the presence of God, we go, not to hear his justice prosecute us but his love plead for us.


## ABOVE THE ANGELS

*Hebrews* 1: 4–14

He was the superior to the angels, in proportion as he had received a more excellent rank than they. For to which of the angels did God ever say: "It is my *Son* that you are; it is I who this day have begotten you"? And again: "I will be to him a Father, and he will be to me a Son." And again, when he brings his honoured one into the world of men, he says: "And let all the angels of God bow down before him." As for the angels, he says: "He who makes his angels winds and his servants a flame of fire." But, as for the Son, he says: "God is your throne for ever and for ever, and the sceptre of righteousness is the sceptre of your kingdom. You have loved justice and hated lawlessness; therefore God has anointed you, even your God, with the oil of exultation above your fellows." And, "You in the beginning, O Lord, laid the foundations of the earth and the heavens are the work of your hands. They shall perish but you remain unalterable. All of them will grow old like a garment, and like a mantle you will fold them up and they will be changed. But you are ever yourself, and your years will not fail." To which of the angels did he ever say: "Sit at my right hand till I make your enemies your footstool"? Are they not all ministering spirits, continually being despatched on service, for the sake of those who are destined to enter into possession of salvation?

IN the previous passage the writer was concerned to prove the superiority of Jesus over all the prophets. Now he is concerned to prove his superiority over the angels. That he thinks it worth while to do this proves the place that belief in angels had in the thought of the Jews of his day. At this time it was on the increase. The reason was that men were more and more impressed with what is called the transcendence of God. They felt more and more the distance and the difference between God and man. The result was that they came to think of the angels as intermediaries between God and man. They came to believe that the angels bridged the gulf between God and man; that God spoke to man through the angels and the angels carried the prayers of man into the presence of God. We see this process particularly in one instance. In the Old Testament the law was given directly by God to Moses, without need of intermediary. But in New Testament times the Jews believed that God gave the law first to angels who then passed it on to Moses, direct communication between man and God being unthinkable (cp. *Acts* 7: 53; *Galatians* 3: 19).

If we look at some of the basic Jewish beliefs about angels we will see them reappearing in this passage. God lived surrounded by his angelic hosts (*Isaiah* 6; 1 *Kings* 22: 19). Sometimes the angels are thought of as God's army (*Joshua* 5: 14f.). Greek for *angels* is *aggeloi* and in Hebrew *mal'akim*. In both languages the meaning is *messenger* as well as *angel*. In fact, *messenger* is the more common meaning. The angels were really the beings who were the instruments in the bringing of God's word and the working of God's will in the universe of men. They were said to be made of an ethereal fiery substance like blazing light. They were created either on the second or the fifth day of creation. They did not eat or drink and they did not beget children. Sometimes they were believed to be immortal, although they could be annihilated by God, but there was another belief about their existence as we shall see. Some of them, the seraphim, the cherubim and the ofanim (-*im* is the plural ending of Hebrew nouns) were always around the throne of God. They were thought of as having more knowledge than men, especially of the future, but they did not possess that knowledge by right but rather because of "what they had heard behind the curtain." They were thought of as the kind of entourage, the *familia*, of God. They were thought of as God's senate; God did nothing without consulting them. For instance, when God said: "Let *us* make man" (*Genesis* 1: 26), it was to the angel senate that he was speaking. Often the angels remonstrated with God and laid objections to his purposes. In particular, they objected to the creation of man and at that time troops of them were annihilated; and they objected to the giving of the law and attacked Moses on his way up Mount Sinai. This was because they were jealous and did not wish to share any of their place or prerogatives with any other creature.

There were millions and millions of angels. It was not till quite late that the Jews assigned names to them. There were, in particular, the seven angels of the presence, who were the archangels. Of these the principal ones were Raphael, Uriel, Phanuel, Gabriel, the angel who brought God's messages to men, and Michael, the angel who presided over the destinies of Israel. The angels had many duties. They brought God's messages to men. In that case they delivered their message and vanished (*Judges* 13:20). They intervened for God in the events of history (2 *Kings* 19:35, 36). There were two hundred angels who controlled the movements of the stars and kept them in their courses. There was an angel who controlled the never-ending succession of the years and months and days. There was an angel, a mighty prince, who was over the sea. There were angels of the frost, the dew, the rain, the snow, the hail, the thunder and the lightning. There were angels who were wardens of hell and torturers of the damned. There were recording angels who wrote down every single word which every man spoke. There were destroying angels and angels of punishment. There was Satan, the prosecuting angel, who on every day except the Day of Atonement continuously brought charges against men before God. There was the angel of death who went out only at God's bidding and who impartially delivered his summons to good and evil alike. Every nation had its guardian angel who had the *prostasia,* the presidency over it. Every individual had his guardian angel. Even little children had their angels (*Matthew* 18:10). So many were the angels that the Rabbis could even say: "Every blade of grass has its angel."

There was one special belief, held only by some, which is indirectly referred to in this passage which we are studying. The common belief was that the angels were immortal; but there were some who believed that they lived only one day. There was a belief in some rabbinic schools that "every day God creates a new company of angels who utter a song before him and are gone." "The angels are renewed every morning and after they have praised God they return to the stream of fire from whence they came." 4 *Esdras* 8: 21 speaks of the God "before whom the heavenly host stand in terror and at thy word change to wind and fire." A rabbinic homily makes one of the angels say: "God changes us every hour. . . . Sometimes he makes us fire, at other times wind." That is what the writer to the Hebrews means when he talks of God making his angels wind and fire.

With this vast angelology there was a very real danger that the angels would come, in men's belief, to intervene between God and them. It was necessary to show that the Son was greater far than they and that he who knew the Son needed no angel to be his intermediary with God. The writer to the Hebrews does it by choosing what are for him a series of proof texts in which the Son is given a higher place than was ever given to any angel. The texts he quotes are: *Psalm* 2: 7; 2 *Samuel* 7: 14; *Psalm* 97: 7 or *Deuteronomy* 32: 43; *Psalm* 104: 4; *Psalm* 45: 7, 8; *Psalm* 102: 26, 27; *Psalm* 110: 1. Some of these texts differ from the versions we know because the writer to the Hebrews was quoting from the Septuagint, the Greek version of the Old Testament, which is not always the same as the original Hebrew from which our versions are translated. Some of the proof texts he chooses seem very strange. For instance, 2 *Samuel* 7: 14 is in the original a simple reference to Solomon and has nothing to do with the Son or the Messiah. *Psalm* 102: 26, 27 is a reference to God and not to the Son. But whenever the early Christians found a text with the word *son* or the word *Lord* they considered themselves quite entitled to take it out of its context and to apply it to Jesus.

There was one danger which the writer to the Hebrews wished at all costs to avoid. The doctrine of angels is a lovely thing; but it has one danger. It introduces a series of beings

other than Jesus through whom man makes approach to God.
In Christianity there is no need for anyone else in between.
Because of Jesus and what he did we have direct access to
God. As Tennyson had it:

> "Speak to him thou for he hears, and Spirit with
>     spirit can meet—
> Closer is he than breathing, and nearer than
>     hands and feet."

The writer to the Hebrews lays down the great truth that we
need no man or supernatural being to bring us into the presence
of God. Jesus Christ has broken every barrier down and
opened a direct way for us to God.


## THE SALVATION WE DARE NOT NEGLECT

*Hebrews* 2: 1-4

> We must, therefore, with very special intensity pay attention to the
> things that we have heard. For, if the word which was spoken
> through the medium of the angels proved itself to be certified as
> valid, and if every transgression and disobedience of it received its
> just recompense, how shall we escape if we neglect so great a
> salvation, a salvation of such a kind that it had its origin in the
> words of the Lord, and was then guaranteed to us by those who
> had heard it from his lips, while God himself added his own witness
> to it by signs and wonders and manifold deeds of power, and by
> giving us each a share of the Holy Spirit, according as he willed it?

THE writer is arguing from the less to the greater. He has in
his mind two revelations. One was the revelation of the law
which came *by the medium of the angels,* that is to say, the Ten
Commandments. Now any breach of that law was followed
by strict and just punishment. The other was the revelation
which came *through the medium of Jesus Christ, the Son.*
Because it came in and through the Son it was infinitely greater
than the revelation of God's truth brought by the angels; and
therefore any transgression of it must be followed by a far more

terrible punishment. If men cannot neglect the revelation which came *through the angels*, how much less can they neglect the revelation which came *through the Son*?

In the first verse there may be an even more vivid picture than there is in the translation which we have used. The two key words are *prosechein* and *pararrein*. We have taken *prosechein* to mean *to pay attention to*, which is one of its commonest meanings. *Pararrein* is a word of many meanings. It is used of something flowing or slipping past; it can be used of a ring that has slipped off the finger; of a particle of food that has slipped down the wrong way; of a topic that has slipped into the conversation; of a point which has escaped someone in the course of an argument; of some fact that has slipped out of the mind; of something that has ebbed or leaked away. It is regularly used of something which has carelessly or thoughtlessly been allowed to become lost.

But both these words have also a nautical sense. *Prosechein* can mean *to moor a ship*; and *pararrein* can be used of a ship which has been carelessly allowed to slip past a harbour or a haven because the mariner has forgotten to allow for the wind or the current or the tide. So, then, this first verse could be very vividly translated: "Therefore, we must the more eagerly anchor our lives to the things that we have been taught lest the ship of life drift past the harbour and be wrecked." It is a vivid picture of a ship drifting to destruction because the pilot sleeps.

For most of us the threat of life is not so much that we should plunge into disaster, but that we should drift into sin. There are few people who deliberately and in a moment turn their backs on God; there are many who day by day drift farther and farther away from him. There are not many who in one moment of time commit some disastrous sin; there are many who almost imperceptibly involve themselves in some situation and suddenly awake to find that they have ruined life for themselves and broken someone else's heart. We must be continually on the alert against the peril of the drifting life.

The writer to the Hebrews characterizes under two headings

the sins for which the law brings its punishment: he calls them *transgression* and *disobedience*. The first of these words is *parabasis,* which literally means *the stepping across a line.* There is a line drawn both by knowledge and by conscience, and to step across it is sin. The second is *parakoē. Parakoē* begins by meaning *imperfect hearing,* as, for instance, of a deaf man. Then it goes on to mean *careless hearing,* the kind which through inattention either misunderstands or fails to catch what has been said. It ends by meaning *unwillingness to hear,* and therefore *disobedience to the voice of God.* It is the deliberate shutting of the ears to the commands and warnings and invitations of God.

The writer to the Hebrews ends this paragraph by stating three ways in which the Christian revelation is unique.

(i) It is unique in its *origin.* It came direct from Jesus himself. It does not consist of guessings and gropings after God; it is the very voice of God himself which comes to us in Jesus Christ.

(ii) It is unique in its *transmission.* It came to the people to whom Hebrews was written from men who had themselves heard it direct from the lips of Jesus. The one man who can pass on the Christian truth to others is he who knows Christ "other than at second hand." We can never teach what we do not know; and we can teach others of Christ only when we know him ourselves.

(iii) It is unique in its *effectiveness.* It issued in signs and wonders and manifold deeds of power. Someone once congratulated Thomas Chalmers after one of his great speeches. "Yes," he said, "but *what did it do?*" As Denney used to say, the ultimate object of Christianity is to make bad men good; and the proof of real Christianity is the fact that it can change the lives of men. The moral miracles of Christianity are still plain for all to see.

## THE RECOVERY OF MAN'S LOST DESTINY

*Hebrews* 2: 5–9

> It was not to angels that he subjected the order of things to come of which we are speaking. Somewhere in scripture someone bears this witness to that fact: "What is man that you remember him? Or the son of man that you visit him? For a little time you made him lower than the angels; you crowned him with glory and honour, you set him over the work of your hands; you subjected all things beneath his feet." The fact that all things have been subjected to him means that nothing has been left unsubjected to him. But as things are, we see that all things are not in a state of subjection to him. But we do see him who was for a little while made lower than the angels, Jesus himself, crowned with glory and honour because of the suffering of his death, a suffering which came to him in order that, by the grace of God, he might drain the cup of death for every man.

THIS is by no means an easy passage of which to grasp the meaning; but when we do, it is a tremendous thing. The writer begins with a quotation from *Psalm* 8: 4–6. If we are ever to understand this passage correctly we must understand one thing—*the whole reference of Psalm* 8 *is to man*. It sings of the glory that God gave to *man*. There is no reference to the Messiah.

There is a phrase in the psalm which makes it difficult for us to grasp that. This is *the son of man*. We are so used to hearing that phrase applied to Jesus that we tend always to take it to refer to him. But in Hebrew *a son of man* always means simply *a man*. We find, for instance, that in the book of the prophet Ezekiel, more than eighty times God addresses Ezekiel as *son of man*. "Son of man, set your face toward Jerusalem" (*Ezekiel* 21: 2). "Son of man, prophesy and say. . . ." (*Ezekiel* 30: 2).

In the psalm quoted here the two parallel phrases. "What is man that you remember him?" and "Or the son of man that you visit him?" are different ways of saying exactly the same thing. The psalm is a great lyric cry of the glory of man as God meant it to be. It is in fact an expansion of the great promise of God at creation in *Genesis* 1 · 28, when he said to man: "Have dominion over the fish of the sea, and over the birds of the air, and over every living thing that moves upon the earth."

The glory of man, incidentally, is even greater than the Authorized Version would lead us to understand. It has: "Thou hast made him a little lower than the angels" (*Psalm* 8: 5). That is a correct translation of the *Greek* but not of the *original Hebrew*. In the original Hebrew it is said that man is made a little lower than the *Elohim*; and *Elohim* is the regular word for *God*. What the psalmist wrote about man really was: "Thou hast made him little less than God," which, in fact, is the translation of the Revised Standard Version. So then this psalm sings of the glory of man, who was made little less than divine and whom God meant to have dominion over everything in the world.

But, the writer to the Hebrews goes on, the situation with which we are confronted is very different. Man was meant to have dominion over everything *but he has not*. He is a creature who is frustrated by his circumstances, defeated by his temptations, girt about with his own weakness. He who should be free is bound; he who should be a king is a slave. As G. K. Chesterton said, whatever else is or is not true, this one ·thing is certain—man is not what he was meant to be.

The writer to the Hebrews goes further on. Into this situation came Jesus Christ. He suffered and he died, and because he suffered and died, he entered into glory. And that suffering and death and glory are all for man, because he died to make man what he ought to be. He died to rid man of his frustration and his bondage and his weakness and to give him the dominion he ought to have. He died to recreate man until he became what he was originally created to be.

In this passage there are three basic ideas. (i) God created man, only a little less than himself, to have the mastery over all things. (ii) Man through his sin entered into defeat instead of mastery. (iii) Into this state of defeat came Jesus Christ in order that by his life and death and glory he might make man what he was meant to be.

We may put it another way. The writer to the Hebrews shows us three things. (i) He shows us *the ideal of what man should be*—kin to God and master of the universe. (ii) He shows us *the actual state of man*—the frustration instead of the mastery, the failure instead of the glory. (iii) He shows us *how the actual can be changed into the ideal through Christ*. The writer to the Hebrews sees in Christ the One, who by his sufferings and his glory can make man what he was meant to be and what, without him, he could never be.

## THE ESSENTIAL SUFFERING

*Hebrews* 2: 10–18

For, in his work of bringing many sons to glory, it was fitting that he for whom everything exists and through whom everything exists, should make the pioneer of salvation fully adequate for his destined work through suffering. For he who sanctifies and they who are sanctified must come of one stock. It is for this reason that he does not hesitate to call them brothers, as when he says: "I will tell your name to my brothers; I will sing hymns to you in the midst of the gathering of your people." And again: "I will put all my trust in him." And again: "Behold me and the children whom God gave to me." The children then have a common flesh and blood and he completely shared in them, so that, by that death of his, he might bring to nothing him who has the power of death, and might set free all those who, for fear of death, were all their lives liable to a slave's existence. For I presume that it is not angels that he helps; but it is the seed of Abraham that he helps. So he had in all things to be made like his brothers, so that he might become a merciful and faithful high priest in the things which pertain to God, to win forgiveness for the sins of his people. For in that he himself was tried and suffered, he is able to help those who are undergoing trial.

HERE the writer to the Hebrews uses one of the great titles of Jesus. He calls him *the pioneer (archēgos) of glory*. The same word is used of Jesus in *Acts* 3: 15; 5: 31; *Hebrews* 12: 2. At its simplest it means *head* or *chief*. So Zeus is the *head* of the gods and a general is the *head* of his army. It can mean a *founder* or *originator*. So it is used of the founder of a city or of a family or of a philosophic school. It can be used in the sense of *source* or *origin*. So a good governor is said to be the *archēgos* of peace and a bad governor the *archēgos* of confusion.

One basic idea clings to the word in all its uses. An *archēgos* is one who begins something in order that others may enter into it. He begins a family that some day others may be born into it; he founds a city in order that others may some day dwell in it; he founds a philosophic school that others may follow him into the truth and the peace that he himself has discovered; he is the author of blessings into which others may also enter. An *archēgos* is one who blazes a trail for others to follow. Someone has used this analogy. Suppose a ship is on the rocks and the only way to rescue is for someone to swim ashore with a line in order that, once the line is secured, others might follow. The one who is first to swim ashore will be the *archēgos* of the safety of the others. This is what the writer to the Hebrews means when he says that Jesus is the *archēgos* of our salvation. Jesus has blazed the trail to God for us to follow.

How was he enabled to become such? The Authorized and Revised Standard Versions say that God made him *perfect* through suffering. The verb translated *make perfect* is *teleioun*, which comes from the adjective *teleios* which is usually translated *perfect*. But in the New Testament *teleios* has a very special meaning. It has nothing to do with abstract and metaphysical and philosophic perfection. It is used, for instance, of an animal which is unblemished and fit to be offered as a sacrifice; of a scholar who is no longer at the elementary stage but mature; of a human being or an animal who is full grown; of a Christian who is no longer on the fringe of the Church but who is baptized. The basic meaning of *teleios* in the New Testament is always that the thing or person so described *fully carries out the purpose for which designed*. Therefore the verb *teleioun* will mean not so much *to make perfect* as *to make fully adequate for the task for which designed*. So, then, what the writer to the Hebrews is saying is that through suffering Jesus was made fully able for the task of being the pioneer of our salvation.

Why should that be?

(i) It was through his sufferings that he was really *identified* with men. The writer to the Hebrews quotes three Old Testament texts as forecasts of this identity with men—*Psalm* 22: 22; *Isaiah* 8: 17; *Isaiah* 8: 18. If Jesus had come into this world in a form in which he could never have suffered, he would have been quite different from men and so no Saviour for them. As Jeremy Taylor said: "When God would save men, he did it by way of a man." It is, in fact, this identification with men which is the essence of the Christian idea of God. When the Greeks thought of their gods they thought of them as Tennyson pictures them in the *Lotos Eaters:*

> "For they lie beside their nectar, and the bolts
>     are hurl'd
> Far below them in the valleys, and the clouds
>     are lightly curl'd
> Round their golden houses, girdled with the
>     gleaming world:
> Where they smile in secret, looking over wasted
>     lands,
> Blight and famine, plague and earthquake,
>     roaring deeps and fiery sands,
> Clanging fights, and flaming towns, and sinking
>     ships, and praying hands."

The basis of the Greek idea of God was *detachment*; the basis of the Christian idea is *identity*. Through his sufferings Jesus Christ identified himself with man.

(ii) Through this identity Jesus Christ *sympathizes* with man. He literally *feels* with them. It is almost impossible to understand another person's sorrows and sufferings unless we have been through them. A person without a trace of nerves has no conception of the tortures of nervousness. A person who is perfectly physically fit has no conception of the weariness of the person who is easily tired or the pain of the person who is never free from pain. A person who learns easily often cannot understand why someone who is slow finds things so difficult.

A person who has never sorrowed cannot understand the pain at the heart of the person into whose life grief has come. A person who has never loved can never understand either the sudden glory or the aching loneliness in the lover's heart. Before we can have sympathy we must go through the same things as the other person has gone through—and that is precisely what Jesus did.

(iii) Because he sympathizes Jesus can really *help*. He has met our sorrows; he has faced our temptations. As a result he knows exactly what help we need; and he can give it.

## GREATER THAN THE GREATEST

*Hebrews* 3: 1–6

> Brothers who are dedicated to God, you who are sharers in heaven's calling, because of all this you must fix your attention on him whom our creed holds to be the apostle and the high priest of God, I mean Jesus, for he was faithful to him who appointed him, just as Moses was in all his house. For he was deemed worthy of more honour than Moses, in so far as the man who builds and equips the house has more honour than the house itself. For every house is built and equipped by someone; but it is God who builds and equips all things. Moses was faithful in all his house, but his role was the role of a servant, and his purpose was to bear witness to the things which some day would be spoken. But Christ is over his house because he is a Son. We are his house if only we keep strong the confidence and pride of our hope to the end.

LET us remember the conviction with which the writer to the Hebrews starts. The basis of his thought is that the supreme revelation of God comcs through Jesus Christ and that only through him has a man real access to God. He began by proving that Jesus was superior to the prophets; he went on to prove that Jesus was superior to the angels; and now he proceeds to prove that Jesus is superior to Moses.

It might at first sight seem that this is an anticlimax. But it was not so for a Jew. For him Moses held a place which was utterly unique. He was the man with whom God had spoken face to face as a man speaks with his friend. He was the direct recipient of the Ten Commandments, the very Law of God. The greatest thing in all the world for the Jew was the Law, and Moses and the Law were one and the same thing. In the second century a Jewish teacher called Rabbi Jose ben Chalafta, commenting on this very passage which declared that Moses was faithful in all his house, said: "God calls Moses faithful in all his house, and thereby he ranked him higher than the ministering angels themselves." For a Jew the step that the writer to the Hebrews takes is the logical and inevitable step in the argument. He has proved that Jesus is greater than the angels; now he must prove that he is greater than Moses who was greater than the angels.

In fact this quotation which is used to tell of the greatness of Moses is proof of the unique position which the Jews assigned to him. "Moses was faithful in all his house." The quotation is from *Numbers* 12: 6, 7. Now the point of the argument in *Numbers* is that Moses differs from all the prophets. To them God makes himself known in a vision; to Moses he speaks "mouth to mouth." To the Jew it would have been impossible to conceive that anyone ever stood closer to God than Moses did, and yet that is precisely what the writer of the Hebrews sets out to prove.

He bids his hearers *fix their attention* on Jesus. The word he uses (*katanoein*) is suggestive. It does not mean simply to look at or to notice a thing. Anyone can look at a thing or even notice it without really seeing it. The word means to fix the attention on something in such a way that its inner meaning, the lesson that it is designed to teach, may be learned. In *Luke* 12: 24 Jesus uses the same word when he says: "*Consider* the ravens." He does not merely mean, "*Look* at the ravens." He means, "Look at the ravens and *understand and learn* the lesson that God is seeking to teach you through them." If we are ever to learn Christian truth, a detached glance is never enough; there must be a concentrated gaze in which we gird up the loins of the mind in a determined effort to see its meaning for us.

In a sense the reason for that is implicit when the writer addresses his friends as *sharers in heaven's calling*. The call that comes to a Christian has a double direction. It is a calling *from* heaven and it is a calling *to* heaven. It is a voice which comes *from* God and calls us *to* God. It is a call which demands concentrated attention because of both its origin and its destination. A man cannot afford to give a disinterested glance to an invitation *to* God *from* God.

When we do fix our attention on Jesus what do we see? We see two things.

(i) We see the great *apostle*. No one else in the New Testament ever calls Jesus an *apostle*. That the writer to the Hebrews does so deliberately is quite clear, because *apostle* is a title he never gives to any man. He keeps it for Christ.

What does he mean when he so uses it? The word *apostolos* literally means *one who is sent forth*. In Jewish terminology it was used to describe the envoys of the Sanhedrin, the supreme court of the Jews. The Sanhedrin sent out *apostoloi* who were clothed with its authority and the bearers of its commands. In the Greek world it frequently meant *ambassador*. So then Jesus is the supreme ambassador of God and an ambassador has two supremely important and relevant characteristics.

(*a*) The ambassador is clothed with all the authority of the king who sends him. On one occasion the king of Syria, Antiochus Epiphanes, invaded Egypt. Rome desired to stop him and sent an envoy called Popillius to tell him to abandon his projected invasion. Popillius caught up with Antiochus on the borders of Egypt and they talked of this and that for they had known each other in Rome. Popillius had not the vestige of an army with him, not even a guard. Finally Antiochus asked him why he had come. Quietly Popillius told him that he had come to tell him that Rome wished him to abandon the invasion and go home. "I will consider it," said Antiochus. Popillius smiled a little grimly; he took his staff and drew a circle in the earth round Antiochus. "Consider it," he said, "and come to your decision before you leave that circle." Antiochus thought for a few seconds and then said: "Very well.

I will go home." Popillius himself had not the slightest force available—but behind him was all the power of Rome. So Jesus came from God and all God's grace and mercy and love and power were in his *apostolos*.

(*b*) The voice of the ambassador is the voice of the king or country who sent him. In a foreign land the British ambassador's voice is the voice of Britain. So Jesus came with the voice of God; in him God speaks.

(ii) Jesus is the great *High Priest*. What does that mean? This is an idea to which the writer to the Hebrews returns again and again. Just now we only set down the fundamental basis of what he means. The Latin for a priest is *pontifex*, which means a *bridge-builder*. The priest is the person who builds a bridge between man and God. To do that he must know both man and God. He must be able to speak to God for men and to speak to men for God. Jesus is the perfect High Priest because he is perfectly man and perfectly God; He can represent man to God and God to man. He is the one person through whom man comes to God and God comes to man.

Wherein then lies the superiority of Jesus over Moses? The picture in the mind of the writer to the Hebrews is this. He thinks of the world as God's house and God's family. We use the word house in a double sense. We use it in the sense of a building and also in the sense of a family. The Greeks used *oikos* in the same double sense. The world, then, is God's house and men are God's family. But he has already shown us the picture of Jesus as the creator of God's universe. Now Moses was only part of God's universe, part of the house. But Jesus is the creator of the house and the creator is bound to stand above the house itself. Moses did not create the law; he only mediated it. Moses did not create the house; he only served in it. Moses did not speak of himself; all that he ever said was only a pointer to the greater things that Jesus Christ would some day say. Moses, in short, was the *servant*; but Jesus was the *Son*. Moses knew a little *about* God; Jesus *was* God. Therein lies the secret of his superiority.

Now the writer to the Hebrews uses another picture. True, the whole world is God's house; but in a special sense the Church is God's House, for in a special sense God brought it into being. That is a picture the New Testament loves (cp. 1 *Peter* 4: 17; 1 *Timothy* 3: 15, and especially 1 *Peter* 2: 5). That building of the Church will stand indestructible only when every stone is firm; that is to say, when its every member is strong in the proud and confident hope he has in Jesus Christ. Each one of us is like a stone in the Church; if one stone is weak the whole edifice is endangered. The Church stands firm only when each living stone in it is rooted and grounded in faith in Jesus Christ.

## WHILE TODAY STILL LASTS

*Hebrews* 3: 7–19

So then, as the Holy Spirit says, "If today you will hear my voice, do not harden your hearts, as in the Provocation, as happened on the day of the Temptation in the wilderness, where your fathers tried to test me, and, in consequence, experienced for forty years what I could do. So my anger was kindled against that generation, and I said, 'Always they wander in their hearts; they do not know my ways.' So I swore in my anger, 'Very certainly they shall not enter in to my rest.' " Have a care, brothers, lest that evil and disobedient heart be in any of you in a state of rebellion against the living God. But keep on exhorting each other day by day, so long as the term "today" can be used, lest any among you be hardened in heart by the seductiveness of sin; for you have become participators in Christ, if indeed you hold fast the beginning of your confidence firm to the end. While it is still possible to hear it being said, "If *today* you will hear my voice," do not harden your hearts as at the Provocation. For who heard and provoked God? Was it not all who came forth from Egypt under the leadership of Moses? Against whom was God's anger kindled for forty years? Was it not against those who had sinned and whose bones lay in the desert? To whom did he swear that they should not enter into his rest, if not to those who were disobedient? Thus we see that it was through disobedience that they could not enter in.

THE writer to the Hebrews has just been striving to prove the unique supremacy of Jesus and now he leaves argument for exhortation. He presses upon his hearers the inevitable consequence of this unique supremacy. If Jesus is so uniquely great, it follows that complete trust and complete obedience must be given to him. If they harden their hearts and refuse to give him their obedient trust the consequences are bound to be terrible.

The way in which he buttresses his argument is for us very difficult for it is doubly allusive. He begins by making a quotation from *Psalm* 95: 7–11. That *Psalm* appeals to those who hear it not to be like the children of Israel but, as the Authorized Version renders it. "Harden not your hearts, as in *the provocation,* in *the day of temptation.*" Now the two phrases, *the provocation* and *the day of temptation* translate two Hebrew words which are *place names*—Massah and Meribah. The whole is a reference to the story told in *Exodus* 17: 1–7 and *Numbers* 20: 1–13. These passages tell of a rebellious incident in the pilgrimage of the children of Israel. They were thirsty in the desert and railed against Moses, regretting that they had ever left Egypt and forswearing their trust in God. In the Numbers version of the story God told Moses to speak to the limestone rock and water would gush forth. But Moses in his anger did not *speak* to the rock; he *struck* it. The water came forth but for this act of distrust and disobedience God declared that Moses would never be allowed to lead the people into the promised land. "Very certainly they shall not enter in to *my rest,*" means, "Very certainly they will not enter into *the Promised Land.*" To wanderers in the desert the Promised Land was the place of rest, and it was often called *the rest* (cp. *Deuteronomy* 12: 9). The point is that the disobedience and the distrust of Israel debarred them from the blessings of God that they might have enjoyed.

The writer to the Hebrews says to his people, "Beware lest you show the same disobedience and distrust of God that your forefathers showed, and that you do not for that reason lose the blessings you might have had, just as they lost theirs." In effect he says, "While there is yet time, while you can still speak of 'today' give God the trust and the obedience that he must have." For the individual "today" means "while life lasts" and the writer to the Hebrews is saying, "While you have the chance, give God the submission you ought to give. Give it to him before your day closes." There are certain great warnings here.

(i) God makes men an offer. Just as he offered the Israelites the blessings of the Promised Land, he offers to all men the blessings of a life which is far beyond the life that men can live without him.

(ii) But to obtain the blessings of God two things are necessary. (*a*) *Trust* is necessary. We must believe that what God says is true. We must be willing to stake our lives on his promises. (*b*) *Obedience* is necessary. It is just as if a doctor were to say to us: "I can cure you if you obey my instructions implicitly." It is just as if a teacher were to say: "I can make you a scholar if you follow my curriculum with absolute fidelity." It is just as if a trainer were to say to an athlete: "I can make you a champion if you do not deviate from the discipline that I lay down." In any realm of life success depends on obedience to the word of the expert. God, if we may put it so, is the expert in life and real happiness depends on obedience to him.

(iii) To the offer of God there is a limit. That limit is the duration of life. We never know when that limit will be reached. We speak easily about "tomorrow" but for us tomorrow may never come. All we have is today. Someone has said: "We should live each day as if it were a lifetime." God's offer must be accepted today; the trust and the obedience must be given today—for we cannot be sure that there will be a tomorrow for us.

Here we have the supreme offer of God, but it is only for perfect trust and full obedience, and it must be accepted now— or it may be too late.

## THE REST WE DARE NOT MISS

*Hebrews* 4: 1–10

It is true that the promise which offers entry into the rest of God still remains for us; but beware lest any of you be adjudged to have missed it. It is indeed true that we have had the good news preached to us, just as those of old had. But the word which they heard was no good to them, because it did not become woven into the very fibre of their being through faith. It is we who have made the decision of faith who are entering into the rest, for of them God said: "I swore in my anger, 'Very certainly they shall not enter into my rest.' " This he said although his works had been finished after the foundation of the world. For somewhere in scripture it speaks thus about the seventh day: "And God rested on the seventh day from all his labours." And it says in the same place: "Very certainly they shall not enter into my rest." Since then it remains that some people must enter into it and since those who in former times had the gospel preached to them did not enter because of their lack of trust, he again defines a day, when in David, after so long a lapse of time, he says, "Today," just as he had said before, "Today if you will hear my voice do not harden your hearts." If Joshua had actually brought them into rest, God would not then after that be speaking about another day. So a Sabbath rest remains for the people of God. He who has entered into this rest has rest from all his works, just as God rested from his works.

In a complicated passage like this it is better to try to grasp the broad lines of the thought before we look at any of the details. The writer is really using the word rest (*katapausis*) in three different senses. (i) He is using it as we would use *the peace of God*. It is the greatest thing in the world to enter into the peace of God. (ii) He is using it, as he used it in 3: 12, to mean *The Promised Land*. To the children of Israel who had wandered so long in the desert the Promised Land was indeed the rest of God. (iii) He is using it of *the rest of God* after the sixth day of creation, when all God's work was completed. This way of using a word in two or three different ways, of teasing at it until the last drop of meaning was extracted from it, was typical of cultured, academic thought in the days when the writer to the Hebrews wrote his letter.

Now let us see the steps of the argument. It will be simpler if we enumerate them one by one.

(i) The promise of the rest of God for his people still abides; the danger is that we fail to reach it.

(ii) The Israelites in the long ago failed to enter into the rest of God. Here the word *rest* is being used in the sense of the settlement of the Promised Land after the wilderness years. The reference is to *Numbers* 13 and 14. These chapters tell how the children of Israel came to the borders of the Promised Land, how they sent out scouts to spy out the land, how ten of the twelve scouts came back with the verdict that it was a good land but that the difficulties of entering into it were insuperable, how Caleb and Joshua alone were for going forward in the strength of the Lord, how the people hearkened to the advice of the cowards, and how the result was that that generation of distrusting cowards were debarred for ever from entering into the rest and the peace of the Promised Land. They did not trust God to bring them through the difficulties that lay ahead; and therefore they never enjoyed the rest they could have had.

(iii) Now the writer switches the meaning of the word *rest*. It is true that these people long ago missed the rest they might have had; but, although they missed it, *the rest remained*. Behind this argument lies one of the favourite conceptions of the Rabbis. On the seventh day, the day after creation had been completed, God rested from his labours. In the creation story in *Genesis* 1 and 2 there is a strange fact. On the first six days of creation it is said that morning and evening came; that is to say, each day had an end and a beginning. But on the seventh day, the day of God's rest, *there is no mention of evening at all*. From this the Rabbis argued that, while the other days came to an end, the day of God's rest had no ending; the rest of God was for ever. Therefore although long ago the Israelites may have failed to enter that rest, it still remained.

(iv) Once again the writer goes back to the meaning of *rest* as the Promised Land. The day came after the forty years wandering in the wilderness when, under Joshua, the people did enter into the Promised Land. Now, the Promised Land was *the rest* and therefore it could be argued that then the promise was fulfilled.

(v) But no, the promise is not fulfilled, because in *Psalm* 95: 7–11 David hears God's voice saying to the people that if they do not harden their hearts they can enter into his *rest*. That is to say, hundreds of years *after* Joshua had led the people into the *rest* of the Promised Land God is *still* appealing to them to enter into his *rest*. There is more to this *rest* than merely entry into the Promised Land.

(vi) So the final appeal comes. God still appeals to men not to harden their hearts but to enter into his rest. God's "today" still exists and the promise is still open; but "today" does not last for ever; life comes to an end; the promise can be missed; therefore, says the writer to the Hebrews: "Here and now through faith enter into the very rest of God."

There is a very interesting question of meaning in verse 1. We have taken the translation: "Beware lest any of you be *adjudged* to have missed the rest of God." That is to say: "Beware lest your disobedience and your lack of faith may mean that you have shut yourselves out from the rest and the peace that God offers you."

That may very well be the correct translation. But there is another and most interesting possibility. The phrase may mean: "Beware lest you think that you have arrived too late in history ever to enjoy the rest of God."

In that second translation there is a warning. It is very easy to think that the great days of religion are past. It is told that a child, on being told some of the great Old Testament stories, said wistfully: "God was much more exciting then." There is a continual tendency in the Church to look back, to believe that God's power is grown less and that the golden days lie behind. The writer to the Hebrews sounds forth a trumpet call. "Never think," he says, "that you have arrived too late in history; never think that the days of great promise and great achievement lie behind. This is still God's 'today.' There is a blessedness for you as great as the blessedness of the saints;

there is an adventure for you as great as the adventure of the martyrs. God is as great today as ever he was."

There are two great permanent truths in this passage.

(i) A word, however great, is of no avail unless it becomes integrated into the person who hears it. There are many different kinds of hearing in this world. There is indifferent hearing, disinterested hearing, critical hearing, sceptical hearing, cynical hearing. The hearing that matters is the hearing that listens eagerly, believes and acts. The promises of God are not merely beautiful pieces of literature; they are promises on which a man is meant to stake his life and dominate his action.

(ii) In the first verse the writer to the Hebrews bids his people *beware* lest they miss the promise. The word we have translated *beware* literally means *to fear* (*phobeisthai*). This Christian fear is not the fear which makes a man run away from a task; nor the fear which reduces him to paralysed inaction; it is the fear which makes him put out every ounce of strength he possesses in a great effort not to miss the one thing that is worth while.


## THE TERROR OF THE WORD

*Hebrews* 4: 11–13

> Let us then be eager to enter into that rest, lest we follow the example of the Israelites and fall into the same kind of disobedience. For the word of God is instinct with life; it is effective; it is sharper than a two-edged sword; it pierces right through to the very division of soul and spirit, joints and marrow; it scrutinizes the desires and intentions of the heart. No created thing can ever remain hidden from his sight; everything is naked to him and is compelled to meet the eyes of him with whom we have to reckon.

THE point of this passage is that the word of God has come to men and is such that it cannot be disregarded. The Jews always had a very special idea about words. Once a word was spoken, it had an independent existence. It was not only a sound with a certain meaning; it was a power which went forth and did things. Isaiah heard God say that the word which went out of his mouth would never be ineffective; it would always do that which he designed it to do.

We can understand something of this if we think of the tremendous effect of words in history. A leader coins a phrase and it becomes a trumpet-call which kindles men to crusades or to crimes. Some great man sends forth a manifesto and it produces action which can make or destroy nations. Over and over again in history the spoken word of some leader or thinker has gone out and done things. If that be so of the words of men, how much more is it so of the word of God.

The writer to the Hebrews describes the word of God in a series of great phrases. *The word of God is instinct with life.* Certain issues are as dead as the dodo; certain books and words have no living interest whatever. Plato was one of the world's supreme thinkers but it is unlikely that there would be any public for Daily Studies in Plato. The great fact about the word of God is that it is a living issue for all men of all times. Other things may pass quietly into oblivion; other things may acquire an academic or antiquarian interest; but the word of God is something that every man must face, its offer something he must accept or reject.

The word of God is *effective*. It is one of the facts of history that wherever men have taken God's word seriously things have begun to happen. When the English Bible was laid bare and the word of God came to the common people, the tremendous event of the Reformation inevitably followed. When people take God seriously they immediately realize that his word is not only something to be studied, not only something to be read, not only something to be written about; *it is something to be done*.

The word of God is *penetrating*. The writer piles up phrases to show how penetrating it is. It penetrates to the division of *soul and spirit*. In Greek the *psuchē*, the *soul*, is the life principle. All living things possess *psuchē*, it is physical life. In Greek the *pneuma*, the *spirit*, is that which is characteristic of man. It is by spirit that man thinks and reasons and looks beyond the

earth to God. It is as if the writer to the Hebrews were saying
that the word of God tests a man's earthly life and his spiritual
existence. He says that the word of God scrutinizes a man's
*desires* and *intentions*. *Desire* (*enthumēsis*) is the *emotional* part
of man, *intention* (*ennoia*) is the *intellectual* part of man. It is
as if he said: "Your emotional and intellectual life must alike
be submitted to the scrutiny of God."

Finally the writer to the Hebrews sums things up. He says
that everything is *naked* to God and *compelled to meet his eyes*.
He uses two interesting words. The word for *naked* is the literal
word (*gumnos*). What he is saying is that as far as men are
concerned we may be able to wear our outward trappings and
disguises; but in the presence of God these things are stripped
away and we have to meet him as we are. The other word is
even more vivid (*tetrachēlismenos*). This is not a common word
and its meaning is not quite certain. It seems to have been used
in three different ways.

(i) It was a wrestler's word and was used for seizing an
opponent by the throat in such a way that he could not move.
We may escape God for long enough but in the end he grips
us in such a way that we cannot help meeting him face to face.
God is one issue that no man can finally evade.

(ii) It was the word that was used for flaying animals.
Animals were hung up and the hide was taken off them. Men
may judge us by our outer conduct and appearance but God
sees into the inmost secrets of our hearts.

(iii) Sometimes when a criminal was being led to judgment or
to execution, a dagger, with point upwards, was so fixed below
his chin that he could not bow his head in concealment but
had to keep it up so that all could see his face and know his
dishonour. When that was done, a man was said to be
*tetrachēlismenos*. In the end we have to meet the eyes of God.
We may avert our gaze from people we are ashamed to meet;
but we are *compelled* to look God in the face. Kermit Eby
writes in *The God in You*: "At some time or other, a man must
stop running from himself and his God—possibly because
there is just no other place to run to." There comes a time

to every man when he has to meet that God from whose eyes nothing ever can be concealed.

## THE PERFECT HIGH PRIEST

*Hebrews* 4: 14–16

> Since, then, we have a high priest, great in his nature, who has passed through the heavens, Jesus, the Son of God, let us hold fast to our creed. For we have not a high priest who is such that he cannot feel with us in our weaknesses; but one who has gone through every temptation, just in the same way as we have, and who is without sin. Let us then confidently approach his throne of grace, that we may receive mercy and find grace to help as need demands.

HERE we are coming to closer grips with the great characteristic conception of Hebrews—that of Jesus as the perfect high priest. His task is to bring the voice of God to man and to usher men into the presence of God. The high priest at one and the same time must perfectly know man and God. That is what this epistle claims for Jesus.

(i) This passage begins by stressing the sheer greatness and absolute deity of Jesus. He is great in his nature, not by honours conferred by men or by any external trappings but, in his own essential being. He has passed through the heavens. That may mean one of two things. In the New Testament we can discern differing uses of *heaven*. It can mean the heaven of the sky and it can mean the heaven of the presence of God. This may mean that Jesus has passed through every heaven that may be and is in the very presence of God. It can mean what Christina Rossetti meant when she said: "Heaven cannot hold him." Jesus is so great that even heaven is too small a place for him. No one ever stressed the sheer greatness of Jesus like the writer to the Hebrews.

(ii) Then he turns to the other side. No one was ever surer of Jesus's complete identity with men. He went through everything that a man has to go through and is like us in all things— except that he emerged from it all completely sinless. Before

we turn to examine more closely the meaning of this, there is
one thing we must note. The fact that Jesus was without sin
means that he knew depths and tensions and assaults of
temptation which we never can know. So far from his battle
being easier it was immeasurably harder. Why? For this
reason—we fall to temptation long before the tempter has put
out the whole of his power. We never know temptation at its
fiercest because we fall long before that stage is reached. But
Jesus was tempted far beyond what we are; for in his case the
tempter put everything he possessed into the assault. Think of
this in terms of pain. There is a degree of pain which the human
frame can stand—and when that degree is passed a person
loses consciousness so that there are agonies of pain he can not
know. It is so with temptation. We collapse in face of temptation; but Jesus went to our limit of temptation and far beyond
it and still did not collapse. It is true to say that he was tempted
in all things as we are; but it is also true to say that no one
was tempted as he was.

(iii) This experience of Jesus had three effects.

(a) It gave him *the gift of sympathy*. Here is something
which we must understand but which we find very difficult.
The Christian idea of God as a loving Father is interwoven
into the very fabric of our mind and heart; but *it was a new
idea*. To the Jew the basic idea of God was that he was *holy*
in the sense of being *different*. In no sense did he share our
human experience and was in fact incapable of sharing it just
because he was God.

It was even more so with the Greeks. The Stoics, the highest
Greek thinkers, said the primary attribute of God was
*apatheia,* by which they meant essential inability to feel
anything at all. They argued that if a person could feel sorrow
or joy it means that some other person was able to influence
him. If so, that other person must, at least for that moment,
be greater than he. No one, therefore, must be able in any
sense to affect God for that would be to make him greater
than God; and so God had to be completely beyond all feeling.
The other Greek school was the Epicureans. They held that

the gods lived in perfect happiness and blessedness. They lived in what they called the *intermundia,* the spaces between the worlds; and they were not even aware of the world.

The Jews had their *different* God; the Stoics, their *feelingless* gods; the Epicureans, their completely *detached* gods. Into that world of thought came the Christian religion with its incredible conception of a God who had deliberately undergone every human experience. Plutarch, one of the most religious of the Greeks, declared that it was blasphemous to involve God in the affairs of this world. Christianity depicted God not so much involved as identified with the suffering of this world. It is almost impossible for us to realize the revolution that Christianity brought about in men's relationship to God. For century after century they had been confronted with the idea of the untouchable God; and now they discovered one who had gone through all that man must go through.

(*b*) That had two results. It gave God *the quality of mercy.* It is easy to see why. It was because God *understands.* Some people have lived a sheltered life; they have been protected from the temptations that come to those for whom life is not easy. Some people have a nature which is easy to control; others have hot passions that make life a perilous thing. The person who has lived the sheltered life and has the non-inflammable nature finds it hard to understand why the other person falls. He is faintly disgusted and cannot help condemning what he cannot understand. *But God knows.* "To know all is to forgive all"—of no one is that truer than he.

John Foster in one of his books tells how he came into his home in this country one day in the thirties to find his daughter in tears before the radio set. He asked her why and found that the news bulletin had contained the sentence—"Japanese tanks entered Canton today." Most people would hear that with at the most a faint feeling of regret. Statesmen may have heard it with grim foreboding; but to most people it did not make so very much difference. Why then was John Foster's daughter in tears? Because she had been born in Canton. To her Canton meant a home, a nurse, a school, friends.

The difference was that *she had been there*. When you have been there it makes all the difference. And there is no part of human experience of which God cannot say: "I have been there." When we have a sad and sorry tale to tell, when life has drenched us with tears, we do not go to a God who is incapable of understanding what has happened; we go to a God who has been there. That is why—if we may put it so—God finds it easy to forgive.

(c) It makes God *able to help*. He knows our problems because he has come through them. The best person to give you advice and help on a journey is someone who has travelled the road before you. God can help because he knows it all.

Jesus is the perfect high priest because he is perfectly God, and perfectly man. Because he has known our life he can give us sympathy, mercy and power. He brought God to men and he can bring men to God.


## AT HOME WITH MAN AND GOD

*Hebrews* 5: 1–10

Every high priest who is chosen from among men is appointed on men's behalf to deal with the things which concern God. His task is to offer gifts and sacrifices for sins, in that he himself is able to feel gently to the ignorant and to the wandering because he himself wears the garment of human weakness. By reason of this very weakness it is incumbent upon him, just as he makes sacrifice for the people, so to make sacrifice for sins on his own behalf also. No one takes this honourable position to himself, but he is called by God to it, just as Aaron was. So it was not Christ who gave himself the glory of becoming high priest; but it was God who said to him: "You are my beloved Son; today I have begotten you." Just so he says also in another passage: "You are a priest for ever according to the order of Melchizedek." In the days when he lived this human life of ours he offered prayers and entreaties to him who was able to bring him safely through death with strong crying and with tears. And when he had been heard because of his reverence, although he was a Son, he learned obedience from the sufferings through which he passed.

When he had been made fully fit for his appointed task, he became
the author of eternal salvation to all who obey him, for he had been
designated by God a high priest after the order of Melchizedek.

Now Hebrews comes to work out the doctrine which is its
special contribution to Christian thought—the doctrine of the
High Priesthood of Jesus Christ. This passage sets out three
essential qualifications of the priest in any age and in any
generation.

(i) A priest is appointed on men's behalf to deal with the
things concerning God. A. J. Gossip used to tell his students
that when he was ordained to the ministry he felt as if the
people were saying to him: "We are for ever involved in the
dust and the heat of the day; we have to spend our time getting
and spending; we have to serve at the counter, to toil at the
desk, to make the wheels of industry go round. We want you
to be set apart so that you can go in to the secret place of God
and come back every Sunday with a word from him to us."
The priest is the link between God and man.

In Israel the priest had one special function, to offer sacrifice
for the sins of the people. Sin disturbs the relationship which
should exist between man and God and puts up a barrier
between them. The sacrifice is meant to restore that relationship and remove that barrier.

But we must note that the Jew was always quite clear, when
thinking at his highest, that the sins for which sacrifice could
atone were *sins of ignorance*. The deliberate sin did not find its
atonement in sacrifice. The writer to the Hebrews himself says:
"For if we sin deliberately after receiving the knowledge of the
truth, *there no longer remains a sacrifice for sins*" (*Hebrews*
10: 26). This is a conviction that emerges again and again in
the sacrificial laws of the Old Testament. Again and again they
begin: "If any one sins unwittingly in any of the things which
the Lord has commanded not to be done . . ." (*Leviticus*
4: 2, 13). *Numbers* 15: 22–31 is a key passage. There the
requisite sacrifices are laid down "if you err unwittingly." But
at the end it is laid down: "That person who does anything

with a high hand ... reviles the Lord ... shall be utterly cut off: his iniquity shall be upon him." *Deuteronomy* 17: 12 lays it down: "The man who acts *presumptuously* ... that man shall die."

The sin of ignorance is pardonable; the sin of presumption is not. Nevertheless we must note that by the sin of ignorance the Jews meant more than simply lack of knowledge. They included the sins committed when a man was swept away in a moment of impulse or anger or passion or mastered by some overmastering temptation and the sins followed by repentance. By the sin of presumption they meant the cold, calculated sin for which a man was not in the least sorry, the open-eyed disobedience of God.

So, then, the priest existed to open the way for the sinner back to God—so long as he wanted to come back.

(ii) The priest must be one with men. He must have gone through men's experiences and his sympathy must be with them. At this point the writer to the Hebrews stops to point out—he will later show that this is one of the ways in which Jesus Christ is superior to any earthly priest—that the earthly priest is so one with men that he is under the necessity of offering sacrifice for his own sin before he offers it for the sins of others. The priest must be bound up with men in the bundle of life. In connection with this he used a wonderful word— *metriopathein*. We have translated it *to feel gently*; but it is really untranslatable.

The Greeks defined a virtue as the mean between two extremes. On either hand there was an extreme into which a man might fall; in between there was the right way. So the Greeks defined *metriopatheia* (the corresponding noun) as the mean between extravagant grief and utter indifference. It was feeling about men in the right way. W. M. Macgregor defined it as "the mid-course between explosions of anger and lazy indulgence." Plutarch spoke of that *patience* which was the child of *metriopatheia*. He spoke of it as that sympathetic feeling which enabled a man to raise up and to save, to spare and to hear. Another Greek blames a man for having no

*metriopatheia* and for therefore *refusing to be reconciled* with
someone who had differed from him. It is a wonderful word.
It means the ability to bear with people without getting
irritated; it means the ability not to lose one's temper with
people when they are foolish and will not learn and do the same
thing over and over again. It describes the attitude to others
which does not issue in anger at their fault and which does
not condone it, but which to the end of the day spends itself
in a gentle yet powerful sympathy which by its very patience
directs a man back to the right way. No man can ever deal
with his fellow-men unless he has this strong and patient,
God-given *metriopatheia*.

(iii) The third essential of a priest is this—no man appoints
himself to the priesthood; his appointment is of God. The
priesthood is not an office which a man takes; it is a privilege
and a glory to which he is called. The ministry of God among
men is neither a job nor a career but a calling. A man ought
to be able to look back and say, not, "I chose this work," but
rather, "God chose me and gave me this work to do."

The writer to the Hebrews goes on to show how Jesus Christ
fulfils the great conditions of the priesthood.

(i) He takes the last one first. Jesus did not choose his task;
God chose him for it. At the Baptism there came to Jesus the
voice which said: "You are my Son; today I have begotten
you" (*Psalm* 2: 7).

(ii) Jesus has gone through the bitterest experiences of men
and understands manhood in all its strength and weakness.
The writer to the Hebrews has four great thoughts about him.

(*a*) He remembers Jesus in Gethsemane. That is what he is
thinking of when he speaks of Jesus's prayers and entreaties,
his tears and his cry. The word he uses for *cry* (*kraugē*) is
very significant. It is a cry which a man does not choose to
utter but is wrung from him in the stress of some tremendous
tension or searing pain. So, then, the writer to the Hebrews
says that there is no agony of the human spirit through which
Jesus has not come. The rabbis had a saying: "There are three
kinds of prayers, each loftier than the preceding—prayer,

crying and tears. Prayer is made in silence; crying with raised voice; but tears overcome all things." Jesus knew even the desperate prayer of tears.

(b) Jesus learned from all his experiences because he met them all with reverence. The Greek phrase for "He learned from what he suffered" is a linguistic jingle—*emathen aph' hōn epathen.* And this is a thought which keeps recurring in the Greek thinkers. They are always connecting *mathein,* to learn, and *pathein,* to suffer. Aeschylus, the earliest of the great Greek dramatists, had as a kind of continual text: "Learning comes from suffering" (*pathei mathos*). He calls suffering a kind of *savage grace* from the gods. Herodotus declared that his sufferings were *acharista mathēmata,* ungracious ways of learning. A modern poet says of the poets:

"We learned in suffering what we teach in song."

God speaks to men in many experiences of life, and not least in those which try their hearts and souls. But we can hear his voice only when we accept in reverence what comes to us. If we accept it with resentment, the rebellious cries of our own heart make us deaf to the voice of God.

(c) By means of the experiences through which he passed, the Authorized Version says that Jesus *was made perfect* (*teleioun*). *Teleioun* is the verb of the adjective *teleios. Teleios* can quite correctly be translated *perfect* so long as we remember what the Greek meant by that perfection. To him a thing was *teleios* if it perfectly carried out the purpose for which it was designed. When he used the word he was not thinking in terms of abstract and metaphysical perfection; he was thinking in terms of *function.* What the writer to the Hebrews is saying is that all the experiences of suffering through which Jesus passed perfectly fitted him to become the Saviour of men.

(d) The salvation which Jesus brought is an *eternal salvation.* It is something which keeps a man safe both in time and in eternity. With Christ a man is safe for ever. There are no circumstances that can pluck him from Christ's hand.

## THE REFUSAL TO GROW UP

*Hebrews* 5: 11–14

> The story which has been laid upon me to tell you about this matter
> is a long story, difficult to tell and difficult to grasp, for your ears
> have become dull. For, indeed, at a stage when you ought to be
> teachers because of the length of time that has passed since you first
> heard the gospel, you still need someone to tell you the simple
> elements of the very beginning of the message of God. You have
> sunk into a state when you need milk and not solid food; for when
> anyone is at the stage of participating in milk feeding, he does not
> really know what Christian righteousness is, for he is only a child.
> For solid food is for those who have reached maturity, those who,
> through the development of the right kind of habit, have reached a
> stage when their perceptions are trained to distinguish between
> good and evil.

HERE the writer to the Hebrews deals with the difficulties which
confront him in attempting to get across an adequate conception of Christianity to his hearers.

He is confronted with two difficulties. First, the full orb of
the Christian faith is by no means an easy thing to grasp nor
can it be learned in a day. Second, the hearing of his hearers
is *dull*. The word he uses (*nōthros*) is full of meaning. It means
slow-moving in mind, torpid in understanding, dull of hearing,
witlessly forgetful. It can be used of the numbed limbs of an
animal which is ill. It can be used of a person who has the
imperceptive nature of a stone. Now this has something to say
to everyone whose business it is to preach and to teach; in fact,
it has something to say to everyone whose business it is to think
and that means that it has something to say to everyone who
is a real person. It often happens that we dodge teaching
something because it is difficult; we defend ourselves by saying
that our hearers would never grasp it. It is one of the tragedies
of the Church that there is so little attempt to teach new
knowledge and new thought. It is true that such teaching is
difficult. It is true that often it means meeting the lethargy of
the lazy mind and the embattled prejudice of the shut mind.

But the task remains. The writer to the Hebrews did not shirk to bring his message, even if it was difficult and the minds of his hearers were slow. He regarded it as his supreme responsibility to pass on the truth he knew.

His complaint is that his hearers have been Christians for many years and are still babes no nearer maturity. The contrast between the immature Christian and the child, between milk and solid food, often occurs in the New Testament (1 *Peter* 2: 2; 1 *Corinthians* 2: 6; 3: 2; 14: 20; *Ephesians* 4: 13ff.). *Hebrews* says that by now they should be teachers. It is not necessary to take that literally. To say that a man was able to teach was the Greek way of saying that he had a mature grasp of a subject. The writer says that they still need someone to teach them *the simple elements* (*stoicheia*) *of Christianity*. This word has a variety of meanings. In grammar it means the letters of the alphabet, the A B C; in physics it means the four basic elements of which the world is composed; in geometry it means the elements of proof like the point and the straight line; in philosophy it means the first elementary principles with which the students begin. It is the sorrow of the writer to the Hebrews that after many years of Christianity his people have never got past the rudiments; they are like children who do not know the difference between right and wrong.

Here he is face to face with a problem which haunts the Church in every generation, that of *the Christian who refuses to grow up*.

(i) The Christian can refuse to grow up in knowledge. He can be guilty of what someone called "the culpable incapacity resulting from the neglect of opportunity." There are people who keep on saying that what was good enough for their fathers is good enough for them. There are Christians in whose faith there has been no development for thirty or forty or fifty or sixty years. There are Christians who have deliberately refused to try to understand the advances that biblical scholarship and theological thought have made. They are grown men and women and yet insist on remaining content with the religious development of a child.

They are like a surgeon who refuses to use the new techniques of surgery, refuses to use the new anaesthetics, refuses to use any new equipment and says: "What was good enough for Lister is good enough for me." They are like a physician who refuses to use any of the new drugs and says: "What I learned as a student fifty years ago is good enough for me." In religious things it is still worse. God is infinite; the riches of Christ are unsearchable; and to the end of the day we should be moving forward.

(ii) There are people who have never grown up in behaviour. It may be forgivable in a child to sulk or to be liable to fits of temper, but there are many adults who are just as childish in their behaviour.

A case of arrested development is always a pathetic thing; and the world is full of people whose religious development has been arrested. They stopped learning years ago and their conduct is that of a child. It is true that Jesus said the greatest thing in the world is the *childlike* spirit; but there is a tremendous difference between the *childlike* and the *childish* spirit. Peter Pan makes a charming play on the stage; but the man who will not grow up makes a tragedy in real life. Let us have a care lest we are still in the religion of childhood when we should have reached the faith of maturity.

## THE NECESSITY OF PROGRESS

*Hebrews* 6: 1–3

So, then, let us leave elementary teaching about Christ behind us and let us be borne onwards to full maturity; for we cannot go on laying the foundations all the time and teaching about repentance from dead works and giving information about washings, about the laying on of hands, about the resurrection from the dead and upon that sentence which lasts to all eternity. God willing, this very thing we will do.

THE writer to the Hebrews was certain of the necessity of progress in the Christian life. No teacher would ever get anywhere if he had to lay the foundations all over again every time he began to teach. The writer to the Hebrews says that his people must be going on to what he calls *teleiotēs.* The Authorized Version translates this word *perfection.* But *teleios,* the adjective, and its kindred words have a technical meaning. Pythagoras divided his students into *hoi manthanontes, the learners,* and *hoi teleioi, the mature.* Philo divided his students into three different classes—*hoi archomenoi, those just beginning, hoi prokoptontes, those making progress,* and *hoi teleiō-menoi, those beginning to reach maturity. Teleiotēs* does not imply complete knowledge but a certain maturity in the Christian faith.

The writer to the Hebrews means two things by this *maturity.* (i) He means something to do with *the mind.* He means that as a man gets older he should more and more have thought things out for himself. He should, for instance, be able to say better who he believes Jesus to be. He should have a deeper grasp, not only of the facts, but also of the significances of the Christian faith. (ii) He means something to do with *life.* As a man grows older there should be more and more of the reflection of Christ upon him. All the time he should be ridding himself of old faults and achieving new virtues. Daily a new serenity and a new nobility should be breaking upon life. As the nameless poet has it:

> "Let me grow lovely, growing old;
>    The many fine things too,
> Laces and Ivory and Gold and Silks,
>    Need not be new.
> And there is healing in old trees,
>    Old streets and glamour old,
> Why may not I, as well as these,
>    Grow lovely, growing old?"

There can be no standing still in the Christian life. It is told that on his pocket Bible Cromwell had a motto written in Latin—*qui cessat esse melior cessat esse bonus*—he who ceases to be better ceases to be good.

ThispassageenablesustoseewhattheEarlyChurch regarded as basic Christianity.

(i) There is *repentance from dead works*. The Christian life begins with *repentance*; and repentance (*metanoia*) is literally *a change of mind*. There is a new attitude to God, to men, to life, to self. It is a repentance from *dead works*. What does the writer to the Hebrews mean by this strange phrase? There are many things that he may mean, and each of them is relevant and suggestive. (*a*) Dead works may be *deeds which bring death*. They may be the immoral, selfish, godless, loveless, soiled actions which lead to death. (*b*) They may be *defiling deeds*. For a Jew to touch a dead body was the greatest defilement; to do so rendered him unclean and barred him from the worship of God until he was cleansed. Dead works may be those which defile a man and separate him from God. (*c*) They may be *works which have no connection with character*. For the Jew life was ritual; if he observed the proper ceremonies at the right time, he was a good man. But none of these things had any effect upon his character. It may be that the writer to the Hebrews means that the Christian has broken away from the meaningless rituals and conventions of life to give himself to the things which deepen his character and develop his soul.

(ii) There is *faith which looks to God*. The first essential in the Christian life is the godward look. The Christian determines his actions not by the verdict of men but by the verdict of God. He looks not to his own achievement for salvation but to the grace of God.

(iii) There is *teaching about washings*. This means that the Christian must realize what baptism really means. The first book of Christian instruction for those about to enter the Church and the first service order book is a little book called *The Didachē, The Teaching of the Twelve Apostles*. It was written about the year A.D. 100 and lays down the regulations for Christian Baptism. Now at this time infant baptism had not yet emerged. Men were coming straight from heathendom and baptism was reception into the Church and confession of faith. *The Didachē* begins with six short chapters on the Christian faith and the Christian life. It begins by telling the candidate for baptism what he ought to believe and how he ought to live. Then in the seventh chapter it goes on:

"Concerning Baptism, baptize in this way. When you have instructed the candidate in all these things, baptize in the name of the Father and of the Son and of the Holy Spirit in running water. If you do not have running water, baptize in any other kind of water. If you cannot baptize in cold water, baptize in warm. If both of these are unobtainable, pour water three times upon the head of the candidate in the name of the Father and of the Son and of the Holy Spirit. Before baptism, let him who is to baptize and him who is to be baptized fast, and let any others who can do so do the same. You must bid him who is to be baptized to fast for two or three days before the ceremony."

That is interesting. It shows that baptism in the early Church was, if possible, by total immersion. It shows that the person to be baptized was either immersed or affused with water three times, in the name of the Father, of the Son and of the Holy Spirit. It shows that baptism was instructed baptism, for the account of the Christian faith and life is to be rehearsed before the sacrament of baptism is carried out. It shows that the candidate for baptism had to prepare not only his mind but also his spirit, for he had to fast beforehand. In the early days no one slipped into the Church without knowing what he was doing. So the writer to the Hebrews says: "At your baptism you were instructed in the basis of the Christian faith. There is no need to go back to that. You must erect a fuller faith on the basis you have already laid down."

(iv) There is *the laying on of hands*. In Jewish practice the laying on of hands had three significances. (*a*) It was the sign of the transference of guilt. The sacrificer laid his hands upon the head of the victim to symbolize the fact that he transferred his guilt to the animal being offered. (*b*) It was the sign of the transference of blessing. When a father blessed his son he laid his hands on the son's head as a token of that blessing. (*c*) It was the sign of setting apart to some special office. A man was ordained to office by the laying on of hands.

In the early Church it always accompanied baptism and was the way in which the Holy Spirit was conveyed to the person newly baptized (*Acts* 8: 17; 19: 6). This is not to be thought of in a material way. In those days the apostles were regarded with reverence because they had actually been the friends of Jesus on earth. It was a thrilling thing to be touched by a man who had actually touched the hand of Jesus. The effect of the laying on of hands depends not on the office of the man who lays on the hands but on his character and his nearness to Christ.

(v) There is *the resurrection from the dead*. Christianity from the beginning was a religion of immortality. It gave a man two worlds in which to live; it taught him that the best was yet to be and thereby made this world the training school for eternity.

(vi) There is *the sentence which lasts to all eternity*. Christianity was from the beginning a religion of judgment. No Christian was ever allowed to forget that in the end he must face God, and that what God thought of him was infinitely more important than what men thought of him.

## CRUCIFYING CHRIST AGAIN

*Hebrews* 6: 4–8

> For it is impossible to renew to repentance those who were once enlightened, those who tasted the free gift from heaven, those who were made sharers in the Holy Spirit, those who tasted the fair word of God and the powers of the age to come, and who then became apostates, for they are crucifying the Son of God again for themselves and are making a mocking show of him. For when the earth has drunk the rain that comes often times upon it and when it brings forth herbage useful to those who cultivate it, it receives a share of blessing from God; but if it produces thorns and thistles it is rejected and is in imminent danger of a curse, and its end is to be appointed for burning.

THIS is one of the most terrible passages in scripture. It begins with a kind of list of the privileges of the Christian life.

The Christian has been *enlightened*. This is a favourite New Testament idea. No doubt it goes back to the picture of Jesus as the Light of the World, the Light that enlightens every man who comes into the world (*John* 1: 9; 9: 5). As Bilney, the martyr said, "When I heard the words, 'Christ Jesus came into the world to save sinners,' it was as if day suddenly broke in the midst of a dark night." The light of knowledge and joy and guidance breaks in upon a man with Christ. So entwined with this idea did Christianity become that *enlightenment* (*phōtismos*) became a synonym for *baptism*, and *to be enlightened* (*phōtizesthai*) became a synonym for *to be baptized*. That is, in fact, the way many people have read this word here; and they have taken this passage to mean that there is no possibility of forgiveness for sins committed after baptism; and there have been times and places in the Church when baptism has been postponed to the moment of death in order to be safe. That idea we shall discuss later.

The Christian has tasted *the free gift that comes from heaven*. It is only in Christ that a man can be at peace with God. Forgiveness is not something he can ever win; it is a free gift. It is only when he comes to the Cross that his burden is rolled away. The Christian is a man who knows the immeasurable relief of experiencing the free gift of the forgiveness of God.

The Christian is *a sharer in the Holy Spirit*. He has in his life a new directive and a new power. He has discovered the presence of a power that can both tell him what to do and enable him to do it.

The Christian has *tasted the fair word of God*. That is another way of saying that he has discovered the truth. It is characteristic of men that instinctively they follow truth as blind men long for light; it is part of the penalty and the privilege of being a man that we can never rest content until we have learned the meaning of life. In God's word we find the truth and the meaning of life.

The Christian *has tasted the powers of the world to come*.

Jew and Christian alike divided time into two ages. There was this present age (*ho nun aiōn*), which was wholly bad; there was the age to come (*ho mellōn aiōn*), which would be wholly good. Some day God would intervene; there would come the shattering destruction and the terrible judgment of the Day of the Lord and then this present age would end and the age to come would begin. But the Christian is a man who here and now is tasting the blessedness of the age which is God's. Even in time he has a foretaste of eternity.

> "Heaven above is softer blue,
>     Earth around is sweeter green;
> Something lives in every hue,
>     Christless eyes have never seen;
> Birds with gladder songs o'erflow,
>     Flowers with deeper beauties shine,
> Since I know, as now I know,
>     I am his, and he is mine."

So the writer to the Hebrews sets out the shining catalogue of Christian blessedness; and then at the end of it there comes like a sudden knell, *who then became apostates.*

What does he mean when he says that it is impossible that those who have become apostates can ever be renewed to repentance? Many thinkers have tried to find a way round this word *impossible* (*adunaton*). Esrasmus held that it was to be taken in the sense of difficult almost to the point of impossibility. Bengel held that what was impossible for man was possible for God, and that we must leave those who have fallen away to the mercy of God's singular love. But when we read this passge we must remember that—*it was written in an age of persecution*: and in any such age apostasy is the supreme sin. In any age of persecution a man can save his life by denying Christ; but every person who does so aims a body-blow at the Church, for it means that he has counted his life and comfort dearer to him than Jesus Christ.

This particular way of putting things has always emerged during and after persecutions. Two hundred years after this came the terrible persecution of the Emperor Diocletian. When

peace came after the storm, the one test some wished to apply
to every surviving member of the Church was: "Did you
deny Christ and so save your life?" And if he had denied his
Lord they would have shut the door on him once and for all.
Kermit Eby tells of a French churchman who, when asked
what he did during the French Revolution, whispered: "I
survived."

This is the condemnation of the man who loved life more
than he loved Christ. It was never meant to be erected into a
doctrine that there is no forgiveness for post-baptismal sin.
Who is any man to say that any other man is beyond the
forgiveness of God? What it is meant to show is the terrible
seriousness of choosing existence instead of loyalty to Christ.

The writer to the Hebrews goes on to say a tremendous thing.
Those who fall away *crucify Christ again*. This is the point of
the great *Quo vadis* legend. It tells how in the Neronic
persecution Peter was caught in Rome and his courage failed.
Down the Appian Way he fled for his life. Suddenly there was
a figure standing in his path. It was Jesus himself. "*Domine,*"
said Peter, "*quo vadis*? Lord, where are you going?" "I am
going back to Rome to be crucified again, this time in your
stead." And Peter, shamed into heroism, turned back to
Rome and died a martyr's death.

Late in Roman history there was an Emperor who tried to
put back the clock. Julian wished to destroy Christianity and
bring back the old gods. His attempt ended in defeat.
Ibsen makes him say: "Where is he now? Has he been at
work elsewhere since *that* happened at Golgotha? . . . Where
is he now? What if *that,* at Golgotha, near Jerusalem, was
but a wayside matter, a thing done, as it were, in the
passing? What if he goes on and on, suffers and dies and
conquers again and again, from world to world?"

There is a certain truth there. At the back of the thought
of the writer to the Hebrews there is a tremendous conception. He saw the Cross as an event which opened a window
into the heart of God. He saw it as showing in a moment of time
the suffering love which is for ever in that heart. The Cross

said to men: "That is how I have always loved you and always will love you. This is what your sin does to me and always will do to me. This is the only way I can ever redeem you."

In God's heart there is always, so long as there is sin, this agony of suffering and redeeming love. Sin does not only break God's law; it breaks his heart. It is true that when we fall away, we crucify Christ again.

Further, the writer to the Hebrews says that when we fall away we make *a mocking show of Christ*. How is that? When we sin the world will say: "So that is all that Christianity is worth. So that is all this Christ can do. So that is all the Cross achieved." It is bad enough that when a Church member falls into sin he brings shame to himself and discredit on his Church; but what is worse is that he draws men's taunts and jeers on *Christ*.

We may note a final thing. It has been pointed out that in the letter to the Hebrews there are four impossible things. There is the impossibility of this passage. The other three are: (i) It is impossible for God to lie (6: 18). (ii) It is impossible that the blood of bulls and goats should take away sin (10: 4). (iii) Without faith it is impossible to please God (11: 6).

## THE BRIGHTER SIDE

*Hebrews* 6: 9–12

Beloved, even if we do speak like this, we are persuaded of better things for you, yes, things that are bound up with salvation. For God is not unjust to forget your work and the love that you displayed in that you have been and still are active in the service of God's dedicated people. We hope with all our hearts that each one of you will display the same zeal to make your hope come true and that you will go on doing so until the end, so that you may not become lazily lethargic but may copy those who through faith and patience inherit the promises.

ONE thing stands out here. This is the only passage in the whole letter where the writer addresses his people as *beloved*. It is precisely after the sternest passage of all that he uses the address of love. It is as if he said to them: "If I did not love you so much I would not speak with such severity." Chrysostom paraphrases the thought this way: "It is better that I should scare you with words than that you should sorrow in deeds." He speaks the truth but, however stern it may be, he speaks it in love.

Further, his very form of speaking shows how individual his love is. "We hope," he says, "that *each one of you* will display the zeal that will make your hope come true." He is not thinking of them as a crowd but as individual men and women. Dr. Paul Tournier in *A Doctor's Casebook* has a paragraph on what he calls *the personalism* of the Bible. "God says to Moses, 'I know you by name' (*Exodus* 33: 17). He says to Cyrus, 'It is I, the Lord, who call you by your name' (*Isaiah* 45: 3). One is struck, on reading the Bible, by the importance in it of personal names. Whole chapters are devoted to long genealogies. When I was young I used to think that they could well have been dropped from the Biblical Canon. But I have since realized that these series of proper names bear witness to the fact that, in the biblical perspective, man is neither a thing nor an abstraction, not a fraction of the mass, as the Marxists see him, but a person." When the writer to the Hebrews wrote with sternness he was not rebuking a Church; he was yearning over individual men and women, as God himself does.

There are two interesting things implicit in this passage.

(i) We learn that even if these people to whom he is writing have failed to grow up in Christian faith and knowledge and even if they have been falling away from their first enthusiasm, they have never given up their practical service to their fellow Christians. There is a great practical truth here. Sometimes in the Christian life we come to times which are arid; the Church services have nothing to say to us, the teaching that we do in Sunday school or the singing that we do in the choir or the service we give on a committee becomes a labour without joy. At such a time there are two alternatives. We can give up our worship and our service, but if we do, we are lost. Or we can go determinedly on with them, and the strange thing is that the light and the romance and the joy will in time come back again. In the arid times, the best thing to do is to go on with the habits of the Christian life and of the Church. If we do, we can be sure that the sun will shine again.

(ii) He tells his people to be imitators of those who through faith and patience inherited the promise. What he is saying to them is: "You are not the first to launch out on the glories and the perils of the Christian faith. Others braved the dangers and endured the tribulations before you and won through." He is telling them to go on in the realization that others have gone through their struggle and won the victory. The Christian is not treading an untrodden pathway; he is treading where the saints have trod.

## THE SURE HOPE

*Hebrews* 6: 13–20

When God made his promise to Abraham, since he was not able to swear by anyone greater, he swore by himself. "Certainly," he said, "I will bless you and I will multiply you." When Abraham had thus exercised patience he received the promise. Men swear by someone who is greater than themselves; and an oath serves for a guarantee beyond all possibility of contradiction. But on this occasion God, in his quite exceptional desire to make clear to the heirs of the promise the unalterable character of his intention, interposed with an oath, so that by two unalterable things, in which it is impossible that God should lie, we, who have fled to him for refuge, might be strongly encouraged to lay hold upon the hope that is set before us. This hope is to us like an anchor, safe and sure, and it enters with us into the inner court beyond the veil, where Jesus has already entered as a forerunner for us, when he became a High Priest for ever after the order of Melchizedek.

GOD made more than one promise to Abraham. *Genesis* 12: 7 tells us of the one made when he called him out of Ur and sent him into the unknown and to the promised land. *Genesis* 17: 5, 6 is the promise of many descendants who would be blessed in him. *Genesis* 18: 18 is a repetition of that promise. But the promise which God swore with an oath to keep comes in *Genesis* 22: 16–18. The real meaning of this first sentence is: "God made many a promise to Abraham, and in the end he actually made one which he confirmed with an oath." That promise was, as it were, doubly binding. It was God's word which in itself made it sure, but in addition it was confirmed by an oath. Now that promise was that all Abraham's descendants would be blessed; therefore it was to the Christian Church, for it was the true Israel and the true seed of Abraham. That blessing came true in Jesus Christ. Abraham certainly had to exercise patience before he received the promise. It was not till twenty-five years after he had left Ur that his son Isaac was born. He was old; Sarah was barren; the wandering was long; but Abraham never wavered from his hope and trust in the promise of God.

In the ancient world the *anchor* was the symbol of hope. Epictetus says: "A ship should never depend on one anchor or a life on one hope." Pythagoras said: "Wealth is a weak anchor; fame is still weaker. What then are the anchors which are strong? Wisdom, great-heartedness, courage—these are the anchors which no storm can shake." The writer to the Hebrews insists that the Christian possesses the greatest hope in the world.

That hope, he says, is one which enters into the inner court beyond the veil. In the Temple the most sacred of all places was the Holy of Holies. The veil was what covered it. Within the Holy of Holies there was held to abide the very presence of God. Into that place only one man in all the world could go, and he was the High Priest; and even he might enter that Holy Place on only one day of the year, the Day of Atonement.

Even then, it was laid down, he must not linger in it for it was a dangerous and a terrible thing to enter into the presence of the living God. What the writer to the Hebrews says is this: "Under the old Jewish religion no one might enter into the presence of God but the High Priest and he only on one day of the year; but now Jesus Christ has opened the way for every man at every time."

The writer to the Hebrews uses a most illuminating word about Jesus. He says that he entered the presence of God as our *forerunner*. The word is *prodromos*. It has three stages of meaning. (i) It means *one who rushes on*. (ii) It means *a pioneer*. (iii) It means a scout who goes ahead to see that it is safe for the body of the troops to follow. Jesus went into the presence of God to make it safe for all men to follow.

Let us put it very simply in another way. Before Jesus came, God was the distant stranger whom only a very few might approach and that at peril of their lives. But because of what Jesus was and did, God has become the friend of every man. Once men thought of him as barring the door; now they think of the door to his presence as thrown wide open to all.

## A PRIEST AFTER THE ORDER OF MELCHIZEDEK

*Hebrews* 7

WE come now to a passage of such paramount importance for the writer to the Hebrews and in itself so difficult to understand that we must deal with it in a special way. Chapter 6 ended with the statement that Jesus had been made a priest for ever after the order of Melchizedek. This priesthood after the order of Melchizedek is the most characteristic thought of Hebrews. Behind it lie ways of thinking and of arguing and of using scripture which are quite strange to us and which we must yet try to understand. It will be best first to collect together all that the writer to the Hebrews has to say about the priesthood after the order of Melchizedek and to read that as a whole before we divide it into shorter passages to study in detail. We shall then try to understand what the writer to the Hebrews was getting at before we study this chapter in detail.

So then, we first collect the passages which deal with this idea. The first is *Hebrews* 5: 1–10.

Every high priest who is chosen from among men, is appointed on men's behalf to deal with the things which concern God. His task is to offer gifts and sacrifices for sins, in that he himself is able to feel gently to the ignorant and to the wandering, because he himself wears the garment of human weakness. By reason of this very weakness it is incumbent upon him, just as he makes sacrifice for the people, so to make sacrifice for sins on his own behalf also. No one takes this honourable position to himself, but he is called by God to it, just as Aaron was. So it was not Christ who gave himself the glory of becoming high priest; but it was he who said to him:

"You are my beloved Son; today I have begotten you."
"You are a priest for ever according to the order of Melchizedek."

In the days when he lived this human life of ours, he offered prayers and entreaties to him who was able to bring him safely through death, with strong crying and with tears. And when he had been heard because of his reverence, although he was a Son he learned obedience from the sufferings through which he passed. When he had been made fully fit for his appointed task, he became the author of eternal salvation to all who obey him, for he had been designated by God *a high priest after the order of Melchizedek*.

The second passage, which deals with this idea is the whole of *Hebrews* 7. So then, first, let us set it down as a whole, remembering that the last verse of *Hebrews* 6 has already said that Jesus had become *a high priest for ever after the order of Melchizedek*.

Now this Melchizedek was King of Salem and priest of the most high God. He met Abraham when he was returning from the smiting of the kings and blessed him and set apart for him a tenth part of the spoils. In the first place, the interpretation of his own name means King of Righteousness and, in the second place, King of Salem means King of Peace. His father is never mentioned nor his mother; nor is there any record of his descent; there is no

mention of the beginning of his days, nor any of the end of his life;
he is exactly like the Son of God; and he remains a priest for ever.

Just see how great this man was—Abraham gave him the tenth
part of the spoils of victory—and Abraham was no less than the
founder of our nation. Now look at the difference—when the sons of
Levi receive their priesthood, they receive an injunction laid down
by the law to exact tithes from the people. That is to say, they exact
tithes from their own brothers, even although they are descendants
of Abraham. But this man, whose descent is not traced from them
at all, exacted tithes from Abraham and actually blessed the man
who had received the promises. Beyond all argument, the lesser is
blessed by the greater. Just so, in the one instance, it is a case of men
who die receiving tithes; but in this instance it is the case of a man
whom the evidence proves to live. Still further—if I may put it this
way—through Abraham, Levi, too, the very man who receives the
tithes, had tithes exacted from him, for he was in his father's body
when Melchizedek met him.

If then the desired effect could have been achieved by the Levitical
priesthood—for it was on the basis of that priesthood that the people
bècame a people of the law—what further need was there to set up
another priest and to call him a priest after the order of Melchizedek,
and not to call him a priest after the order of Aaron? Once the
priesthood was altered, of necessity there follows an alteration of the
law too, for the person of whom the statements are made belongs to
another tribe altogether, from which no one ever served at the altar.
It is obvious that it was from Judah that our Lord sprang and, with
regard to that tribe, Moses said nothing about priests. And certain
things are still more abundantly clear—if a different priest is set up,
a priest after the order of Melchizedek, a priest who became so, not
according to the law of a mere human injunction but according to
the power of a life that is indestructible—for the witness of scripture
in regard to this is: "You are a priest for ever after the order of
Melchizedek"—if all that is so, two things emerge. On the one hand
there emerges the cancellation of the previous injunction because of
its own weakness and uselessness (for the law never achieved the
effect which it was designed to produce) and, on the other hand,
there emerges the introduction of a better hope through which we
can come near to God.

And inasmuch as it happened with an oath—for the Levitical
priests are made priests without an oath but he with an oath, because

scripture says of him: "The Lord swore and will not repent of it, 'You are a priest for ever'"—in so far Jesus has become the surety of a better covenant. Further, of the Levitical priests more and more were made priests because they were prevented from continuing permanently by death, whereas he has a priesthood which will never pass away because he remains for ever. For that very reason it is in every possible way and for all time that he, who is for ever alive, can save those who come to God through him.

We needed such a high priest—one who is holy, one who has never hurt any man, one who is stainless, one who is different from sinners, one who has become higher than the heavens. He does not need, as the high priests do, daily first to offer sacrifices for his own sins and then thereafter for the sins of the people. For he did this once and for all when he offered himself. For the law appointed as high priests men subject to weakness; but the word of the oath, which came after the law, appointed one who is a Son who is fully equipped to carry out his office for ever.

THESE are the passages in which the writer to the Hebrews describes Jesus as *a priest after the order of Melchizedek*. Now let us see just what he is trying to say when he uses that conception.

We must begin by understanding the general position from which he starts. He starts with the basic idea that *religion is access to God*. It was to make that access to God possible that two things existed. First, *the law*. The basic idea of the law is that so long as a man faithfully observes its commandments he is in a position of friendship with God and the door to his presence is open to him. But men cannot keep the law and therefore their fellowship with God and their access to his presence are interrupted. It was exactly to deal with that situation of estrangement that the second thing existed, *the priesthood and the whole sacrificial system*. The Latin word for *priest* is *pontifex* which means a *bridge-builder*; the priest was a man whose function was to build a bridge between men and God by means of the sacrificial system. A man broke the law; his fellowship with God was interrupted and his access to God was barred; by the offering of the correct sacrifice that breach of the law was atoned for and so the fellowship was restored and the barrier removed.

That was the theory of the matter. But in practice life showed that that was precisely what the priesthood and the sacrificial system could not do. There was no escaping the human estrangement from God which followed sin; and the problem was that not all the efforts of the priesthood and not all the sacrifices could restore that lost relationship. It is therefore the argument of the writer to the Hebrews that what is needed is a new and a different priesthood and a new and effective sacrifice. He sees in Jesus Christ the only High Priest who can open the way to God; and he calls the priesthood of Jesus a priesthood *after the order of Melchizedek*.

He got that idea from two passages in the Old Testament. The first was *Psalm* 110: 4 where it is written:

"The Lord has sworn and will not change his mind, 'You are a priest for ever after the order of Melchizedek'."

The second is *Genesis* 14: 17–20 where the story of the original Melchizedek is told.

And the king of Sodom went out to meet him (Abram) at the Valley of Shaveh (that is, the King's Valley). And Melchizedek king of Salem brought out bread and wine; he was priest of God most High. And he blessed him and said, "Blessed be Abram by God Most High, maker of heaven and earth; and blessed be God most High, who has delivered your enemies into your hand!" And Abram gave him a tenth of everything.

The writer to the Hebrews is here doing what any skilled Jewish Rabbi might do and following the rabbinic method of interpretation. To understand that method we must understand two things.

(i) To the scholarly Jew any passage of scripture had *four* meanings to which he gave four different names. (*a*) First, there was *Peshat*, which is the literal and factual meaning. (*b*) Second, there was *Remaz*, which is the suggested meaning. (*c*) Third, there was *Derush*, which is the meaning arrived at after long and careful investigation. (*d*) Fourth, there was *Sod*, which is the allegorical or inner meaning. To the Jew the most important meaning by far was *Sod*, the inner meaning. He was not nearly so much interested in the factual meaning of a passage as in the allegorical and mystical meaning which could be extracted from it, even although it might have no connection whatever with the literal meaning. It was quite permissible, and in fact the regular practice, to take things right out of their context and read into them meanings which we would consider fantastic and quite unjustified. That is what the writer to the Hebrews is doing here.

(ii) Second, it is essential to note that the Jewish interpreters considered themselves completely justified in arguing not only from the *utterances* but also from the *silences* of scripture. An argument could be built, not only on what scripture said but also on what it did not say. In fact the writer to the Hebrews bases his argument in this passage at least as much on what scripture did not say about Melchizedek as on what it did.

Now let us see how the quality of the priesthood after the order of Melchizedek differs from the quality of the ordinary Aaronic priesthood.

(i) *Melchizedek has no genealogy*; he is without father and without mother (*Hebrews* 7: 3). Note straight away that this is one of the arguments drawn from the *silence* of scripture which does not provide Melchizedek with any genealogy. This was unusual for two reasons. (*a*) It is the reverse of the habitual practice of Genesis. Genealogies are a feature of Genesis where long lists of a man's ancestors constantly occur. But Melchizedek arrives on the scene, as it were, from nowhere. (*b*) Far more important—it is the reverse of the rules which governed the Aaronic priesthood which depended entirely on descent. Under Jewish law a man could not under any circumstances become a priest unless he could produce a certificated pedigree going back to Aaron. Character and ability had nothing to do with it; the one essential was that pedigree. When the Jews came back to Jerusalem from exile certain priestly families could not produce their genealogical records and were therefore debarred from the priesthood for ever (*Ezra* 2: 61–63; *Nehemiah* 7: 63–65). On the other hand, if a man could produce

a pedigree reaching back to Aaron, apart only from certain
specified physical blemishes nothing on earth could stop him
being a priest. Genealogy was literally everything.

So then, the first difference between the two priesthoods was
this—*the Aaronic priesthood depended on genealogical descent;
the priesthood of Melchizedek depended on personal qualification alone*. Melchizedek's priesthood was based on what *he was,*
not on what *he had inherited*. As one scholar puts it—the
difference was between a claim based on *legality* and a claim
based on *personality*.

(ii) *Hebrews* 7: 1–3 collects further qualities about Melchizedek. The name *Melchizedek* literally means *King of Righteousness*. The word *Salem* means *peace*; therefore he was also *King
of Peace*. We have seen that he has no genealogy. Again the
writer to the Hebrews draws on the silence of scripture. We
are told of no time when Melchizedek began or ended his
priesthood; we are told of no time when he was born or died.
Therefore he had no beginning and has no end; and his
priesthood lasts for ever.

From this we gather five great qualities in the priesthood of
Melchizedek. (*a*) It is a priesthood of *righteousness*. (*b*) It is a
priesthood of *peace*. (*c*) It is a *royal* priesthood, for
Melchizedek was a king. (*d*) It is *personal and not inherited*
because he has no genealogy. (*e*) It is *eternal,* because he has
no birth or death, and his priesthood has no beginning or end.

(iii) Supposing all this to be true, how can it be proved that
the priesthood of Melchizedek is superior to the Aaronic? The
Hebrews seizes on two points in the Genesis story about
Melchizedek.

First, there is the saying that *Abraham gave Melchizedek
tithes of all*. The priests also exact tithes; but there are two
differences. The priests tithe their brethren, their fellow Jews;
and they tithe them as a result of legal enactment. But
Melchizedek tithed Abraham who had no racial connection
with him whatsoever and was in fact the founder of the Jewish
nation; further, he exacted the tithes not because the law gave
him the right to do so but because of an unquestionable

personal right. Obviously that set him far above the ordinary priesthood.

Second, there is the saying that *Melchizedek blessed Abraham*. It is always the superior who blesses the inferior; therefore Melchizedek was superior to Abraham although Abraham was the founder of the Jewish race and the unique recipient of the promises of God. That indeed gives Melchizedek a place than which none could be higher.

A. B. Bruce thus sums up the points in which Melchizedek was superior to the ordinary Levitical priesthood. (*a*) He tithed Abraham and was therefore superior to him. Abraham was one of the patriarchs; the patriarchs are superior to their descendants; therefore Melchizedek is greater than the descendants of Abraham; the ordinary priests are the descendants of Abraham; therefore Melchizedek is greater than they. (*b*) Melchizedek is greater than the sons of Levi because they exacted tithes by legal enactment but he did it as a right he personally possessed given to him by no man. (*c*) The Levites received tithes as mortal men; he received them as one who lives for ever (*Hebrews* 7: 8). (*d*) Levi, to whom the Israelites paid tithes, may be said to have paid tithes to Melchizedek, because he was Abraham's grandson and was therefore in Abraham's body at the time Abraham paid tithes.

(iv) *Hebrews* 7: 11 onwards shows *wherein the superiority of the new priesthood lay*.

(*a*) *The very fact that a new priesthood was promised* (*Hebrews* 7: 11) *shows that the old one was inadequate*. If the old priesthood had fulfilled the function of bringing men to the presence of God there would have been no need for any other. Further, the introduction of the new priesthood was a revolution. According to the law, all priests must belong to the tribe of *Levi*; but Jesus was from the tribe of *Judah*. This shows that the whole old system was superseded. Something greater than the law had come.

(*b*) *The new priesthood was for ever* (*Hebrews* 7: 15–19). Under the old system the priests died and there was no permanency; but now there had come a priest who lives for ever.

(*c*) *The new priesthood was introduced by an oath of God.*
*Psalm* 110: 4 says: "The Lord has sworn and will not change
his mind 'You are a priest for ever after the order of
Melchizedek'." Clearly God does not swear lightly. He never
introduced the ordinary priesthood like that. This was something new.

(*d*) *The new priest offered no sacrifice for himself* (*Hebrews*
7: 27). The ordinary priest always had to make sacrifice for
*his own* sin before he could do so for the sins of the people.
But Jesus Christ, the new High Priest, was sinless and needed
no sacrifice for himself.

(*e*) *The new priest did not need endlessly to repeat sacrifices*
(*Hebrews* 7: 27). He made the one perfect sacrifice, which never
needs to be made again because it has for ever opened the way
to the presence of God.

We now sum up briefly the ideas in the mind of the writer to
the Hebrews when he thinks of Jesus in terms of the High Priest
after the order of Melchizedek. To make it clearer we set out
only the great salient ideas without the side-lines.

(i) Jesus is the High Priest, whose priesthood depends not
on any genealogy but on himself alone.

(ii) Jesus is the High Priest who lives for ever.

(iii) Jesus is the High Priest who himself is sinless and never
needs to offer any sacrifice for his own sin.

(iv) Jesus is the High Priest who in the offering of himself
made the perfect sacrifice which once and for all opened the
way to God. No more sacrifice need be made.

Having seen the general ideas in the mind of the writer to the
Hebrews concerning Jesus as a priest after the order of
Melchizedek, we now turn to this passage in detail and study
it in sections.

## THE TRUE KING AND THE TRUE PRIEST

*Hebrews* 7: 1-3

Now this Melchizedek was King of Salem and priest of the most
high God. He met Abraham when he was returning from the smiting

of the kings and blessed him, and Abraham set apart for him a tenth part of the spoils. In the first place, the interpretation of his own name means King of Righteousness and, in the second place, King of Salem means King of Peace. His father is never mentioned nor his mother; nor is there any record of his descent; there is no mention of the beginning of his days nor any of the end of his life; he is exactly like the Son of God; and he remains a priest for ever.

As we have seen, the two passages on which the writer to the Hebrews founds his argument are *Psalm* 110: 4 and *Genesis* 14: 18–20. In the old Genesis story Melchizedek is a strange and almost eerie figure. He arrives out of the blue; there is nothing about his life, his birth, his death or his descent. He simply arrives. He gives Abraham bread and wine which to us, reading the passage in the light of what we know, sounds so sacramental. He blesses Abraham. And then he vanishes from the stage of history with the same unexplained suddenness as he arrived. There is little wonder that in the mystery of this story the writer to the Hebrews found a symbol of Christ.

Melchizedek from his name was King of Righteousness and from his realm King of Peace. The order is at once significant and inevitable. *Righteousness must always come before peace.* Without righteousness there can be no such thing as peace. As Paul has it in *Romans* 5: 1: "Therefore since we are *justified* by faith, we have *peace* with God." As he has it again in *Romans* 14: 17: "The kingdom of God is . . . *righteousness, peace* and joy." The order is always the same—first righteousness and then peace.

It may well be said that all life is a search for peace, and also that men persist in looking for it in the wrong place.

(i) Men look for peace in *escape*. But the trouble about escape is that it is always necessary to return. A. J. Gossip draws a picture of a slatternly woman who lived in a slatternly house. She leaves her home one afternoon and goes to a cinema. For an hour or two she escapes into the glamour and the luxury of the world of the film—and then she must go back home. It is escape all right—but there is the inevitable return.

W. M. Macgregor tells of an old woman who lived in a terrible slum in Edinburgh called the Pans. Every now and again she would grow disgusted with the surroundings in which she lived and would make a tour of her friends, extracting a penny or two from each. With the proceeds she would get helplessly drunk. When others remonstrated with her she would answer: "Do you grudge me my one chance to get out of the Pans with a sup of whisky?" Again it was escape—but she, too, had to return. It is always possible to find some kind of peace by the route of escape, but it is never a lasting peace. Dr. Johnson used to insist that a man should have a hobby, for he held that a man should have as many retreats for his mind as possible. But even there there is the necessity to return. Escape is not wrong; sometimes it is necessary if health and sanity are to be preserved; but it is always a palliative and never a cure.

(ii) There is the peace of *evasion*. Many a man seeks peace by refusing to face his problems—he pushes them into the back of his mind and seeks to draw down the blind on them. There are two things to be said about that. The first is that no one ever solved a problem by refusing to look at it. However much we evade it, it is still there. And problems are like diseases— the longer we refuse to face them the worse they get. We may well come to a stage when the disease is incurable and the problem insoluble. The second thing is maybe even more serious. Psychology tells us that there is a part of the mind which never stops thinking. With our conscious minds we may be evading a problem but our subconscious mind is teasing away at it. The thing is there like a piece of hidden shrapnel in the body; and it can ruin life. So far from bringing peace, evasion is most destructive of peace.

(iii) There is the way of *compromise*. It is possible to arrive at some kind of peace by arriving at some kind of compromise. It is in fact one of the commonest methods of the world. We can seek peace by toning down some principle or by an uneasy agreement in which neither party is fully satisfied. Kermit Eby says that we may compromise for long enough but the time comes when a man must stand up and be counted if he wants to sleep at nights. Compromise means the loose ends of things unsolved. Compromise, therefore, inevitably means tension, even if a more or less hidden tension; tension inevitably means a gnawing worry; and therefore compromise really is the enemy of peace.

(iv) There is the way of *righteousness,* or, to put it otherwise, the way of *the will of God.* There is no real peace for any man until he has said: "Thy will be done." But once he has said that, peace floods his soul. It happened even to Jesus. He went into the Garden with a soul under such tension that he sweated blood. In the Garden he accepted God's will and came out at peace. To take the way of righteousness, to accept God's will is to remove the root of dispeace and find the way to lasting peace.

The writer to the Hebrews piles up words to show that Melchizedek has no descent. He does this to contrast the new priesthood of Jesus Christ with the old Aaronic priesthood. A Jew could not be a priest unless he could trace an unbroken descent from Aaron; but if he could trace such a descent nothing could stop him being a priest. If a priest married and his bride-to-be was the daughter of a priest, she must produce her pedigree for four generations back; if she was not the daughter of a priest, she must produce her pedigree for five generations back. It is the odd and almost incredible fact that the whole Jewish priesthood was founded on genealogy. Personal qualities did not enter into it at all. But Jesus Christ was the true priest, not because of what he inherited but because of what he was.

Some of the words Hebrews piles up here are amazing. He says that Jesus was *without descent* (*agenealogētos*). That is a word that, so far as we know, no Greek writer ever used before. It may well be that in his eagerness to stress the fact that Jesus's power did not depend on descent, he invented it. It is very likely a new word to describe a new thing. He says that Melchizedek was without father (*apatōr*) and without mother (*amētōr*). These words are very interesting. They have certain uses in secular Greek. They are the regular description of waifs and strays and of people of low pedigree. They contemptuously dismiss a man as having no ancestry. More, *apatōr* has a technical legal use in the contemporary Greek of the papyri. It is the word which is used on legal documents, especially on birth certificates, for *father unknown* and, therefore, *illegitimate*. So, for instance, there is a papyrus which speaks of: "Chairēmōn, *apatōr,* father unknown, whose mother is Thasēs." It is amazing that the writer to the Hebrews took words like this to stress his meaning. The Christian writers had a strange way of redeeming words as well as men and women. No phrase seemed too strong to the writer to the Hebrews to insist upon the fact that Jesus's authority was in himself and came from no man.

## THE GREATNESS OF MELCHIZEDEK

*Hebrews* 7: 4–10

> Just see how great this man was—Abraham gave him the tenth of the spoils of victory—and Abraham was no less than the founder of our nation. Now look at the difference—when the sons of Levi receive their priesthood, they receive an injunction laid down by the law to exact tithes from the people. That is to say, they exact tithes from their own brothers, even although they are descendants of Abraham. But this man, whose descent is not traced through them at all, exacted tithes from Abraham and actually blessed the man who had received the promises. Beyond all argument the lesser is blessed by the greater. Just so, in the one instance, it is the case of men who die receiving tithes; but in this instance, it is the case of a man whom the evidence proves to live. Still further, if I may put it this way, through Abraham Levi, too, the very man who receives the tithes, had tithes exacted from him, for he was in his father's body when Melchizedek met him.

THE writer to the Hebrews is here concerned to prove the superiority of the Melchizedek priesthood to the ordinary. He proceeds on the matter of tithes, because Abraham had given to Melchizedek a tenth part of the spoils of his victory. The law of tithes is laid down in *Numbers* 18: 20, 21. There Aaron is told that the Levites will have no actual territory in the promised land laid down for them but that they are to receive a tenth part of everything for their services in the tabernacle. "And the Lord said to Aaron, 'You shall have no inheritance in their land, neither shall you have any portion among them: I am your portion and your inheritance among the people of Israel. To the Levites I have given every tithe in Israel for an inheritance, in return for their service which they serve, their service in the tent of meeting.' "

So now in a series of contrasts the writer to the Hebrews works out the superiority of Melchizedek over the Levitical priests. He makes five different points. (i) The Levites receive tithes from the people and that is a right that only they enjoy. Melchizedek received tithes from Abraham although he was not a member of the tribe of Levi. It could be argued that while that put him on a level with the Levites, it does not prove that he was superior to them. So our writer adds four other points. (ii) The Levites tithe their brother Israelites; Melchizedek was not an Israelite but a stranger; and it was no ordinary Israelite from whom he received tithes but from no less a person than Abraham, the founder of the nation. (iii) It was due to a legal enactment that the Levites have the right to exact tithes; but Melchizedek received tithes for the sake of what he was personally. He had such personal greatness that he needed no legal enactment to entitle him to receive tithes. (iv) The Levites receive tithes as dying men; but Melchizedek lives for ever. (v) Finally he produces a curious argument for which he apologizes before he states it. Levi was a direct descendant of Abraham and the only man legally entitled to receive tithes. Now, if he was a direct descendant of Abraham it means that he was already in Abraham's body. Therefore when Abraham paid tithes to Melchizedek, Levi also paid them, being included in Abraham's body, the final proof that Melchizedek was superior to him. It is an extremely odd argument but it was no doubt convincing enough to those to whom it was addressed.

Strangely enough, this argument enshrines the great truth that what a man does reacts on his descendants. If he commits some sin, he may transmit to his descendants either the tendency to that sin or some actual physical handicap because of it. If he builds up excellence of character, he transmits a fine inheritance to those who come after. Levi, on the argument of the writer to the Hebrews, was affected by what Abraham did. Therein, amidst the fantastics of the rabbinic argument, remains the truth that no man lives to himself but transmits something of himself to those who follow after.

## THE NEW PRIEST AND THE NEW WAY

*Hebrews* 7: 11–20

If, then, the desired effect could have been achieved by the Levitical priesthood—for it was on the basis of it that the people became a people of the law—what further need was there to set up another priest, and to call him a priest after the order of Melchizedek, and not to call him a priest after the order of Aaron? Once the priesthood was altered, of necessity there follows an alteration of the law, too, for the person of whom the statements are made belongs to another tribe altogether, from which no one ever served at the altar. It is obvious that it was from Judah that our Lord sprang, and with regard to that tribe Moses said nothing about priests. And certain things are still more abundantly clear—if a different priest is set up, a priest after the order of Melchizedek, a priest who has become so, not according to the law of a mere human injunction but according to the power of life that is indestructible—for the witness of scripture in regard to this is: "You are a priest for ever after the order of Melchizedek"—if all that is so, two things emerge. On the one hand, there emerges the cancellation of the previous injunction because of its own weakness and uselessness (for the law never achieved the effect it was designed to produce) and, on the other hand, there emerges the introduction of a better hope through which we can come near to God.

As we read this passage we have to remember the basic idea of religion which never leaves the mind of the writer to the

Hebrews. To him religion is access to God's presence as friends, with nothing between us and him. The old Jewish religion was designed to produce that fellowship in two ways. First, by obedience to the law. Let a man obey the law and he was the friend of God. Second, it was recognised that such perfect obedience was out of the question for any man; and so the sacrificial system came in. When a man was guilty of a breach of the law, the requisite sacrifice was supposed to heal that breach. When the writer to the Hebrews says that the people became a people of the law on the basis of the Levitical priesthood, he means that without the Levitical sacrifices to atone for breaches of it, the law would have been completely impossible. But, in fact, the system of Levitical sacrifices had proved ineffective to restore the lost fellowship between God and man. So then a new priesthood was necessary, the priesthood after the order of Melchizedek.

He says that that priesthood differed from the old in that it was not dependent on merely human—*fleshly* is the word in the Greek—injunctions, but on the power of a life that is indestructible. What he means is this. Every single regulation that governed the old priesthood had to do with the priest's physical body. To be a priest he must be a pure descendant of Aaron. Even then there were one hundred and forty-two physical blemishes which might disqualify him; some of them are detailed in *Leviticus* 21: 16–23. The ordination ceremony is outlined in *Leviticus* 8. (i) He was bathed in water so that he would be ceremonially clean. (ii) He was clothed in the four priestly garments—the linen knee breeches, the long linen garment woven in one piece, the girdle round the breast, and the bonnet or turban. (iii) He was anointed with oil. (iv) He was touched on the tip of the right ear, his right thumb and his right great toe with the blood of certain sacrifices which had been made. Every single item in the ceremony affects the priest's body. Once he was ordained he had to observe so many washings with water, so many anointings with oil; he had to cut his hair in a certain way. From beginning to end the Jewish priesthood was dependent on physical things. Character, ability, personality had nothing to do with it. But the new priesthood was dependent on *a life that is indestructible.* Christ's priesthood depended not on physical things but on what he was in himself. Here was a revolution; it was no longer outward ceremonies and observances that made a priest but inward worth.

Further, there was another great change which had fundamental implications. The law was definite that all priests must belong to the tribe of *Levi*; they must be descendants of Aaron; but Jesus belonged to the tribe of *Judah.* Therefore, the very fact that he was the supreme priest meant that the law was cancelled; it was wiped out. The word used for cancellation is *athetēsis*; that is the word used for annulling a treaty, for abrogating a promise, for scoring a man's name off the register, for rendering a law or regulation inoperative. The whole paraphernalia of the ceremonial law was wiped out in the priesthood of Jesus.

Finally, Jesus can do what the old priesthood never could— he can give us access to God. How does he do that? What is it that keeps a man from having access to God? (i) There is *fear.* So long as a man is terrified of God he can never be at home with him. Jesus came to show men the infinite tender love of the God whose name is Father—and the awful fear is gone. We know now that God wants us to come home, not to punishment but to the welcome of his open arms. (ii) There is *sin.* Jesus on his Cross made the perfect sacrifice which atones for sin. Fear is gone; sin is conquered; the way to God is open to men.

## THE GREATER PRIESTHOOD

*Hebrews* 7: 21–25

And in so far as it happened with an oath—for the Levitical priests are made priests without an oath, but he with an oath, because scripture says of him, "The Lord swore and will not repent of it, 'You are a priest for ever' "—in so far Jesus has become the surety

of a better covenant. Further, of the Levitical priests more and more
were made priests because they were prevented from continuing
permanently by death, whereas he has a priesthood which will never
pass away, because he remains for ever. For that very reason, it is in
every possible way and for all time that he who is for ever alive to
make intercession for us can save those who come to God
through him.

THE writer to the Hebrews is still accumulating his proofs
that the priesthood after the order of Melchizedek, the priesthood after the order of Melchizedek was confirmed by the oath
he brings forward other two proofs.

First, he stresses the fact that the institution of the priesthood after the order of Melchizedek was confirmed by the oath
of God while the ordinary priesthood was not. The reference
is to *Psalm* 110: 4: "*The Lord hath sworn,* and will not change
his mind, 'You are a priest for ever after the order of
Melchizedek.' " The very idea of God taking an oath is
startling. Long ago Philo saw this. He pointed out that the only
reason for taking an oath is because a man's bare word may
be disbelieved; and the oath is to guarantee that his word is
true. God never needs to do that because it is impossible that
his word should ever be disbelieved. If, therefore, God ever
confirms a statement by an oath, that statement must be of
extraordinary importance. So then it is possible that the
ordinary priesthood can pass away; but the priesthood of Jesus
Christ can never pass away; because God has sworn an oath
that it will last for ever.

Because this priesthood has been confirmed by an oath,
Jesus is *the surety of a better covenant.* Let us remember that
the function of the priest and of all religion is to open a way
of access to God. Here we come upon the word *covenant.* We
shall soon have to examine it in more detail. It is sufficient at
the moment to say that a covenant is in essence an agreement
between two people that if one faithfully performs certain
undertakings, the other will respond in a certain way.

There was an ancient covenant between Israel and God that
if the Israelites faithfully obeyed God's law, the way of access

to his friendship would always be open to them. We see the
nation entering into that covenant in *Exodus* 24: 1–8. We see
Moses taking the book of the law and reading it to the people;
and we see the people responding with the words: "All that
the Lord has spoken we will do, and we will be obedient"
(*Exodus* 24: 7). The old agreement was based on obedience to
the law; and the agreement could be kept open only when the
priests kept on making sacrifice for every breach of the law.

Jesus is the surety of a new and a better covenant, a new
kind of relationship between man and God. The difference
is this—the old covenant was based on law and justice and
obedience; the new covenant is based on love and on the
perfect sacrifice of Jesus Christ. The old covenant was based
on man's achievement; the new covenant is based on God's
love.

What does the writer to the Hebrews mean by saying that
Jesus is the *surety* (*egguos*) of this new covenant? An *egguos*
is one who gives security. It is used, for instance, of a person
who guarantees someone else's overdraft at a bank; he is surety
that the money will be paid. It is used for someone who goes
bail for a prisoner; he guarantees that the prisoner will appear
at the trial. The *egguos* is one who guarantees that some
undertaking will be honoured.

So, then, what the writer to the Hebrews means is this.
Someone might say: "How do you know that the old covenant
is no longer operative? How do you know that access to God
now depends, not on man's achievement of obedience but
simply on the welcoming love of God?" The answer is: "Jesus
Christ guarantees that it is so. He is the surety who promises
that God's love will be forthcoming, if only we take him at
his word." To put it in the simplest possible way—we must
believe that when we look at Jesus in all his love we are seeing
what God is like.

The writer to the Hebrews introduces a second proof of the
superiority of the priesthood of Jesus. There was no permanency about the old priesthood. Those who were priests
died and had to be replaced; but the priesthood of Jesus is for

ever. The thing that matters in this passage is the overtones and implications of the almost untranslatable words the writer uses.

He says that the priesthood of Jesus is one *that will never pass away* (*aparabatos*). *Aparabatos* is a legal word. It means *inviolable*. A judge lays down that his decision must remain *aparabatos, unalterable*. It means *non-transferable*. It describes something which belongs to one person and cannot ever be transferred to anyone else. Galen, the medical writer, uses it to describe absolute scientific law which can never be violated, the principles on which the very universe is built and holds together. So then the writer to the Hebrews says that the priesthood of Jesus is something which can never be taken from him, is something that no one else can ever possess, is something that is as lasting as the laws which hold the universe together. Jesus is and will always remain the only way to God. The writer to the Hebrews uses another wonderful word about Jesus and says of him that *he remains for ever* (*paramenein*). That verb has two characteristic flavours. First, it means *to remain in office*. No one can ever take the office of Jesus from him; to all eternity he remains the introducer of men to God. Second, it means *to remain in the capacity of a servant*. Gregory of Nazianzen provides in his will that his daughters will *remain* (*paramenein*) with their mother so long as she is alive. They are to stay with her and be her help and support. The papyri talk of a girl who must *remain* (*paramenein*) in a shop for three years in order to discharge by her work a debt that she cannot pay. There is a papyrus contract which says that a boy, who is being bound as an apprentice, must *remain* (*paramenein*) with his master for as many days extra as he has played truant. When the writer to the Hebrews says that Jesus *remains for ever*, there is wrapped up in that phrase the amazing thought that *Jesus is for ever at the service of men*. In eternity as he was in time Jesus exists to be of service to mankind. That is why he is the complete Saviour. On earth he served men and gave his life for them; in Heaven he still exists to make intercession for them. He is the priest for ever, the one who is for ever opening the door to the friendship of God and is for ever the great servant of mankind.

## THE HIGH PRIEST WE NEED

*Hebrews* 7: 26–28

> We needed such a high priest—one who is holy, one who never hurt any man, one who is stainless, one who is different from sinners, one who has become higher than the heavens. He does not need, as the high priests do, daily first to offer sacrifices for his own sins and thereafter for the sins of the people. For he did this once and for all when he offered himself. For the law appointed as high priests men subject to weakness, but the word of the oath, which came after the law, appointed one who is a Son who is fully equipped to carry out his office for ever.

STILL the writer to the Hebrews is filled with the thought of Jesus as high priest. He begins this passage by using a series of great words and phrases to describe him.

(i) He says that Jesus is *holy* (*hosios*). This word is used of Jesus in *Acts* 2: 27 and 13: 35; it is used of the Lord in *Revelation* 15: 4 and 16: 5; it is used of the Christian bishop in *Titus* 1: 8; it is used of the hands that a man must present to God in prayer in 1 *Timothy* 2: 8. Behind it there is always one special idea. It always describes the man who faithfully does his duty to God. It describes a man, not so much as he appears before his fellow-men but as he appears before God. *Hosios* has in it the greatest of all goodnesses, the goodness which is pure in the sight of God.

(ii) He says that Jesus *never hurt any man* (*akakos*). *Kakia* is the Greek word for evil; and *akakos* describes the man who is so cleansed of evil that there is nothing left in him but good. It describes a man in his effect upon his fellow-men. Sir Walter Scott claimed for himself as a writer that he never corrupted any man's morals or unsettled any man's faith. The man who is *akakos* is so cleansed that his presence

is like an antiseptic and in his heart there is nothing but the
loving kindness of God.

(iii) He says that Jesus is *stainless* (*amiantos*). *Amiantos*
describes the man who is absolutely free from any of the
blemishes which might make it impossible for him to draw
near to God. The blemished victim cannot be offered to God;
the defiled man cannot approach him; but the one who is
*amiantos* is fit to enter into God's presence.

(iv) He says that Jesus is *different from sinners*. This phrase
does not mean that Jesus was not really a man. He was
different from sinners in that, although he underwent all a
man's temptations, he conquered them all and emerged
without sin. The difference between him and other men lies
not in the fact that he was not fully man, but in the fact that he
was manhood at its highest and its best.

(v) He says that Jesus *was made higher than the heavens*.
In this phrase he is thinking of the exaltation of Jesus. If
the last phrase stresses the perfection of his manhood, this
one stresses the perfection of his godhead. He who was
a man amongst men is also he who is exalted to the right hand
of God.

The writer to the Hebrews now introduces another aspect
in which the priesthood of Jesus is far superior to the
Levitical. Before the High Priest could offer sacrifice for the
sins of the people, he had first to offer sacrifice *for his own sins,*
for he was a sinful man.

It is of the Day of Atonement that the writer is specially
thinking. This was the great day when atonement was made
for all the sins of the people, the day on which the High
Priest performed his supreme function. Usually it was the
only day in the year when he personally carried out the
sacrifices. On ordinary days they were left to the subordinate
priests but on the Day of Atonement the High Priest himself
officiated.

The very first item on the ritual of that day was a sacrifice
for the sins of the High Priest himself. He washed his hands
and his feet; he put off his gorgeous robes; he clothed himself

in spotless white linen. There was brought to him a bullock which he had purchased with his own money. He laid both hands on the bullock's head to transfer his sin to it; and thus he made confession: "Ah, Lord God, I have committed iniquity; I have transgressed; I have sinned, I and my house. O Lord, I beseech thee, cover over the sins and transgressions which I have committed, transgressed and sinned before thee, I and my house."

The greatest of all the Levitical sacrifices began with a sacrifice for the sins of the High Priest. That was a sacrifice Jesus never needed to make, for he was without sin. The Levitical High Priest was a sinful man offering animal sacrifices for sinful people; Jesus was the sinless Son of God offering himself for the sin of all men. It was the law which had appointed the Levitical High Priest; it was the oath of God which gave Jesus his office; and because he was what he was, the sinless Son of God, he was equipped for his office as no human High Priest could ever be.

Now the writer to the Hebrews does what he so often does. He drops a marker to indicate the direction he is going to take. He says of Jesus that *he offered himself*. Two things were necessary in a sacrifice. There was the priest and there was the sacrifice. With long and intricate argument the writer to the Hebrews has proved that Jesus was the perfect High Priest; now he is going to move on to another thought. Not only was Jesus the perfect High Priest, *he was also the perfect offering*. Jesus alone could open the way to God because he was the perfect High Priest and he offered the one perfect sacrifice—himself.

There is much in this argument which for us is difficult to understand. It speaks and thinks in terms of ritual and ceremony long since forgotten; but one eternal thing remains. Man seeks the presence of God; his sin has erected a barrier between him and God but he is restless until he rests in God; and Jesus alone is the priest who can bring the offering that can open the way back to God for men.

## THE WAY TO REALITY

*Hebrews* 8: 1–6

The pith of what we are saying is this—it is just such a high priest we possess, a priest who has taken his seat at the right hand of the throne of majesty in the heavens, a high priest who is a minister of the sanctuary and of the real tabernacle, which the Lord, and not man, founded. For every high priest is appointed to offer gifts and sacrifices. It is therefore necessary that he should have something which he might offer. If then he had been upon earth, he would not even have been a priest, for there already exist those who offer the gifts the law lays down, men whose service is but a shadowy outline of the heavenly order, just as Moses received instructions when he was about to complete the tabernacle— "See," it says, "that you do everything according to the pattern that was shown to you on the mountain." But, as things are, he has obtained a more excellent ministry, in so far as he is also the mediator of a better covenant, a covenant which was enacted on the basis of superior promises.

THE writer to the Hebrews has finished describing the priesthood after the order of Melchizedek in all its glory. He has described it as the priesthood which is for ever, without beginning and without end; the priesthood that God confirmed with an oath; the priesthood that is founded on personal greatness and not on any legal appointment or racial qualification; the priesthood which death cannot touch; the priesthood which is able to offer a sacrifice that never needs to be repeated; the priesthood which is so pure that it has no necessity to offer sacrifice for any sins of its own. Now he makes and underlines his great claim. "It is," he says, "a priest precisely like that that we have in Jesus."

He goes on to say two things about Jesus. (i) He took his seat at the right hand of the throne of majesty in the heavens. That is the final proof of his *glory*.

> "The highest place that heaven affords
> Is his, is his by right,
> The King of kings, and Lord of lords,
> And heaven's eternal light."

There can be no glory greater than that of the ascended

and exalted Jesus. (ii) He says that Jesus is a minister of the sanctuary. That is the proof of his *service*. He is unique both in majesty and in service.

Jesus never looked on majesty as something to be selfishly enjoyed. One of the greatest of the Roman Emperors was Marcus Aurelius; as an administrator he was unsurpassed. He died at fifty-nine, having worked himself to death in the service of his people. He was one of the Stoic saints. When chosen to succeed in due time to the imperial power, his biographer Capitolinus tells us, "he was appalled rather than overjoyed, and when he was told to move to the private house of Hadrian, the Emperor, it was with reluctance that he departed from his mother's villa. And when the members of the household asked him why he was sorry to receive the royal adoption, he enumerated to them the toils which sovereignty involved." Marcus Aurelius saw kingship in terms of service and not of majesty.

Jesus is the unique example of divine majesty and divine service combined. He knew that he had been given his supreme position, not jealously to guard it in splendid isolation, but rather to enable others to attain to it and to share it. In him the supreme majesty and the supreme service met.

Now there enters into the picture a thought that was never far from the mind of the writer to the Hebrews. Religion to him, remember, was *access to God*; therefore the supreme function of any priest was to open the way to God for men. He removed the barriers between God and man; he built a bridge across which man could go into the presence of God. But we could put this another way. Instead of talking about *access to God* we might talk about *access to reality*. Every religious writer has to search for terms which his readers will understand. He has to present his message in language and in thoughts which will get home because they are familiar or at least will strike a chord in the reader's mind. The Greeks had a basic thought about the universe. They thought in terms of two worlds, the real and the unreal. They believed that this world of space and time was only a pale copy of the real world. That was the basic doctrine of Plato, the greatest of all the Greek thinkers. He believed in what he called *forms*. Somewhere there was a world where there was laid up the perfect forms of which everything in this world is an imperfect copy. Sometimes he called the forms *ideas*. Somewhere there is the idea of a chair of which all actual chairs are imperfect copies. Somewhere there is an idea of a horse of which all actual horses are inadequate reflections. The Greeks were fascinated by this conception of a real world of which this world is only a flickering, imperfect copy. In this world we walk in shadows; somewhere there is reality. The great problem in life is how to pass from this world of shadows to the other world of realities. That is the idea of which the writer to the Hebrews makes use.

The earthly Temple is a pale copy of the real Temple of God; earthly worship is a remote reflection of real worship; the earthly priesthood is an inadequate shadow of the real priesthood. All these things point beyond themselves to the reality of which they are the shadows. The writer to the Hebrews even finds that idea in the Old Testament itself. When Moses had received from God instructions about the construction of the tabernacle and all its furnishings, God said to him: "And see that you make them after the pattern for them, which is being shown you on the mountain" (*Exodus* 25: 40). God had shown Moses the real pattern of which all earthly worship is the ghost-like copy. So then the writer to the Hebrews says that the earthly priests have a service which is but a *shadowy outline* of the heavenly order. For *shadowy outline* he combines two Greek words, *hupodeigma,* which means *a specimen,* or, still better, a sketch-plan, and *skia*, which means *a shadow*, a reflection, a phantom, a silhouette. The earthly priesthood is unreal and cannot lead men into reality; but Jesus *can*. We can say that Jesus leads us into the presence of God or we can say that Jesus leads us into reality; it means the same thing. When the writer to the Hebrews spoke of *reality* he was using language that his contemporaries used and understood.

In the highest that this world can offer there is some imperfection. It never quite reaches what we know the thing might be. Nothing we ever experience or achieve here quite reaches the ideal that haunts us. The real world is beyond. As Browning had it: "A man's reach should exceed his grasp, or what's a heaven for?" Call it heaven, call it reality, call it the idea or the form, call it God—it is beyond.

As the writer to the Hebrews saw it, only Jesus can lead us out of the frustrating actuality into the all-satisfying real. So he calls him the *mediator,* the *mesitēs. Mesitēs* comes from *mesos,* which, in this case, means *in the middle.* A *mesitēs* is, therefore, *one who stands in the middle between two people and brings them* together. When Job is desperately anxious that somehow he should be able to put his case to God, he cries out hopelessly: "There is no umpire, *mesitēs,* between us" (*Job* 9: 33). Paul calls Moses the *mesitēs* (*Galatians* 3: 19) in that he was the one between who brought the law from God to men. In Athens in classical times there was a body of men—all citizens in their sixtieth year—who could be called upon to act as mediators when there was a dispute between two citizens, and their first duty was to effect a reconciliation. In Rome there were *arbitri.* The judge settled points of law; but the *arbitri* settled matters of equity; and it was their duty to bring disputes to an end. Further, in legal Greek a *mesitēs* was a *sponsor,* a *guarantor* or a *surety.* He went bail for a friend who was on trial; he guaranteed a debt or an overdraft. The *mesitēs* was the man who was willing to pay his friend's debt to make things right again.

The *mesitēs* is the man who stands between and brings together two other parties in reconciliation. Jesus is our perfect *mesitēs*; he stands between us and God. He opens the way to reality and to God and is the only person who can effect reconciliation between man and God, between the real and the unreal. In other words, Jesus is the only person who can bring us real life.

## THE NEW RELATIONSHIP

*Hebrews* 8: 7–13

For, if the first covenant, which is so well known to you, had been faultless there would have been no need to seek any place for a second one. It is to censure them that he says: "Look you the days are coming, says the Lord, when I will consummate a new covenant with the house of Israel and with the house of Judah. It will not be the same as the covenant which I made with their fathers, when I laid my hand on them to lead them forth from the land of Egypt; this must be so because they did not abide by my covenant, and I let them go their own way, says the Lord. It will be different because this is the covenant which I will make with the house of Israel after these days, says the Lord. I will put my laws into their mind and I will inscribe them upon their hearts. I will be to them all that a God should be to them, and they will be to me all that a people should be to me. And no one will teach his fellow-citizen and no one will teach his brother, saying, 'Know the Lord,' for all will know me, small and great alike, because I will graciously forgive their iniquities and I will not remember their sins any more." In that he calls the covenant *new*, he has rendered the first covenant out of date; and that which is out of date and ageing into decay is near to final obliteration.

HERE Hebrews begins to deal with one of the great biblical ideas—that of *a covenant*. In the Bible the Greek word that is always used for a covenant is *diathēkē* and there was a special reason for the choice of this rather unusual word. Ordinarily a covenant is an agreement entered into by two people. It is dependent on conditions on which they mutually agree; and if either should break the conditions the covenant becomes void. It is sometimes used in that simple sense in the Old Testament. For instance, it is used of the *league* that the Gibeonites wished to make with Joshua (*Joshua* 9: 6); of the forbidden *league* with the Canaanites (*Judges* 2: 2); and of David's *covenant* with Jonathan (1 *Samuel* 23: 18). But its distinctive use is to describe the relationship between Israel and God. "Take heed to yourselves, lest you forget the *covenant* of the Lord your God" (*Deuteronomy* 4: 23). In the New Testament the word is also used to describe the relationship between God and man.

But there is a strange point which requires explanation. For all normal uses the Greek word for an agreement is *sunthēkē* which is the word for a marriage covenant or bond and for an agreement between two states. Further, in all normal Greek *diathēkē* means not an agreement, but *a will*. Why should the New Testament use this word for a covenant? The reason is this—*sunthēkē* always describes an agreement entered into on equal terms. The parties to a *sunthēkē* are on the one level and each can bargain with the other. But God and man do not meet on equal terms. In the biblical sense of a covenant, the whole approach comes from God. Man cannot bargain with God; he cannot argue about the terms of the covenant; he can only accept or reject the offer that God makes.

The supreme example of such an agreement is *a will*. The conditions of a will are not made on equal terms. They are made entirely by one person, the testator, and the other party cannot alter them but can only accept or refuse the inheritance offered.

That is why our relationship to God is described as a *diathēkē*, a covenant for the terms of which only one person is responsible. That relationship is offered us solely on the initiative and the grace of God. As Philo said: "It is fitting for God to give and for a wise man to receive." When we use the word covenant, we must always remember that it does not mean that man made a bargain with God on equal terms. It always means that the whole initiative is with God; the terms are his and man cannot alter them in the slightest.

The ancient covenant, so well known to the Jews, was the one made with the people after the giving of the law. God graciously approached the people of Israel. He offered them a unique relationship to himself; but that relationship was entirely dependent on the keeping of the law. We see the Israelites accepting that condition in *Exodus* 24: 1–8. The argument of the writer to the Hebrews is that that old

covenant is done away with and that Jesus has brought a
new relationship with God.

In this passage we can distinguish certain marks of the
new covenant which Jesus brought.

(i) The writer begins by pointing out that the idea of a new
covenant is not something revolutionary. It is already there in
*Jeremiah* 31: 31–34, which he quotes in full. Further, the
very fact that scripture speaks of the new covenant shows
that the old was not fully satisfactory. Had it been, a new
covenant would never have needed to be mentioned.
Scripture looked to a new covenant and therefore itself
indicated that the old covenant was not perfect.

(ii) This covenant will not only be new; *it will be different
in quality and in kind*. In Greek there are two words for *new*.
*Neos* describes a thing as being new in point of time. It
might be a precise copy of its predecessors, but since if it has
been made after the others, it is *neos*. *Kainos* means not only new
in point of time, but new in point of quality. A thing which
is simply a reproduction of what went before may be *neos*
but it is not *kainos*. This covenant which Jesus introduces is
*kainos*, not merely *neos*; it is different in quality from the
old covenant. The writer to the Hebrews uses two words
to describe the old covenant. He says that it is *gēraskōn*,
which means not only *ageing,* but *ageing into decay*. He
says that it is near to *aphanismos*. *Aphanismos* is the word
that is used for wiping out a city, obliterating an inscription,
or abolishing a law. So the covenant which Jesus brings is
new in quality and completely cancels the old.

(iii) Wherein is this covenant new? *It is new in its scope*.
It is going to include *the house of Israel and the house of
Judah*. One thousand years before this, in the days of
Rehoboam, the kingdom had split apart, into Israel with the
ten tribes and Judah with the two, and these two sections
had never come together again. The new covenant is going
to unite that which has been divided; in it the old enemies
will be at one.

(iv) *It is new in its universality*. All men would know God from the least to the greatest. That was something quite new. In the ordinary life of the Jews there was a complete cleavage. On the one hand there were the Pharisees and the orthodox who kept the law; on the other hand there were what were contemptuously called The People of the Land, the ordinary people who did not fully observe the details of the ceremonial law. They were completely despised. It was forbidden to have any fellowship with them; to marry one's daughter to one of them was worse than to throw her to a wild beast; it was forbidden to go on a journey with them; it was even forbidden, as far as it was possible, to have any trade or business dealings with them. To the rigid observers of the law the ordinary people were beyond the pale. But in the new covenant these breaches would no longer exist. All men, wise and simple, great and small, would know the Lord. The doors which had been shut were thrown wide open.

(v) There is one even more fundamental difference. The old covenant depended on obedience to an externally imposed law. *The new covenant is to be written upon men's hearts and minds.* Men would obey God not because of the terror of punishment, but because they loved him. They would obey him not because the law compelled them unwillingly to do so, but because the desire to obey him was written on their hearts.

(vi) It will be a covenant *which will really effect forgiveness.* See how that forgiveness is to come. *God said that he would be gracious to their iniquities and would forget their sins.* Now it is all of God. The new relationship is based entirely on his love. Under the old covenant a man could keep this relationship to God only by obeying the law; that is, by his own efforts. Now everything is dependent not on man's efforts, but solely on the grace of God. The new covenant puts men into relationship with a God who is still a God of justice but whose justice has been swallowed up in his love. The most tremendous thing about the new covenant is that it makes man's relationship to God no longer dependent on man's obedience but entirely dependent on God's love.

One thing remains to say. In Jeremiah's words about the new covenant there is no mention of sacrifice. It would seem that Jeremiah believed that in the new age sacrifice would be abolished as irrelevant; but the writer to the Hebrews cannot think except in terms of the sacrificial system and very shortly he will go on to speak of Jesus as himself the perfect sacrifice, whose death alone made the new covenant possible for men.

## THE GLORY OF THE TABERNACLE

*Hebrews* 9: 1–5

> So, then, the first tabernacle, too, had its ordinances of worship and its holy place, which was an earthly symbol of the divine realities. For the first tabernacle was constructed and in it there was the lampstand and the table with the shewbread, and it was called the Holy Place. Behind the second curtain there was that part of the tabernacle which was called the Holy of Holies. It was approached by means of the golden altar of incense, and it had in it the ark of the covenant, which was covered all over with gold. In the ark there was the golden pot with the manna and Aaron's rod which budded and the tables of the covenant. Above it there were the cherubim of glory, overshadowing the mercy seat; but this is not the place to speak about all these things in detail.

THE writer to the Hebrews has just been thinking of Jesus as the one who leads us into reality. He has been using the idea that in this world we have only pale copies of what is truly real. The worship that men can offer is only a ghost-like shadow of the real worship which Jesus, the real High Priest, alone can offer. But even as he thinks of that his mind goes back to the Tabernacle (the Tabernacle, remember, not the Temple). Lovingly he remembers its beauty; lovingly he lingers on its priceless possessions. And the thought in his mind is this—if earthly worship was as beautiful as this, what must the true worship be like? If all the loveliness of the Tabernacle was only a shadow of reality, how surpassingly lovely the reality must be. He does not tell of the Tabernacle in detail; he only alludes to certain of its treasures. This was all he needed to do because his readers knew its glories and had them printed on their memories. But we do not know them; therefore, let us see what the beauty of the earthly Tabernacle was like, always remembering that it was only a pale copy of reality.

The main description of the Tabernacle in the wilderness is in *Exodus* 25–31 and 35–40. God said to Moses: "Make me a sanctuary that I may dwell in their midst" (*Exodus* 25: 8). It was constructed out of the freewill offerings of the people (*Exodus* 25: 1–7), who gave with such lavish generosity that a halt had to be called to their giving (*Exodus* 36: 5–7).

*The Court of the Tabernacle* was 150 feet long and 75 feet wide. It was surrounded by a curtain-like fence of fine, twined linen 7½ feet high. The white linen stood for the wall of holiness that surrounds the presence of God. The curtain was supported by twenty pillars on the north and south sides, and by ten on the east and west sides; and the pillars were set in sockets of brass and had tops of silver. There was only one gate. It was on the east side and it was 30 feet wide and 7½ feet high. It was made of fine, twined linen wrought with blue and purple and scarlet. In the court there were two things. There was the *Brazen Altar*, 7½ feet square and 4½ feet high and made of acacia wood sheathed in brass. Its top was a brazen grating on which the sacrifice was laid; and it had four horns to which the offering was bound. There was *The Laver*. The laver was made from the brass mirrors of the women (glass mirrors did not exist at that time) but its dimensions are not given. The priests bathed themselves in the water in it before they carried out their sacred duties.

*The Tabernacle* itself was constructed of forty-eight acacia beams, 15 feet high and 2 feet 3 inches wide. They were overlaid with pure gold and rested in sockets of silver. They were bound together by outside connecting rods and by a wooden tie-beam which ran through their centre. The Tabernacle was divided into two parts. The first—two-thirds of the whole—was *The Holy Place*; the inner part—one-third of the whole—a cube 15 feet on each side, was *The Holy of Holies*. The curtain which hung in front of *The Holy Place* was supported on five brass pillars and made of fine linen wrought in blue, purple and scarlet.

*The Holy Place* contained three things. (i) There was *The Golden Lampstand*. It stood on the south side; it was beaten out of a talent of solid gold; the lamps were fed with pure olive oil, and were always lit. (ii) On the north side stood *The Table of the Shewbread*. It was made of acacia wood covered with gold; it was 3 feet long, 1½ feet wide and 2 feet 3 inches high. On it there were laid every Sabbath twelve loaves made of the finest flour, in two rows of six. Only the priests could eat these loaves when they were removed. They were changed every Sabbath. (iii) There was *The Altar of Incense*. It was of acacia wood sheathed in gold; it was 1½ feet square and 3 feet high. On it incense, symbolising the prayers of the people rising to God, was burned every morning and evening.

In front of *The Holy of Holies* there was *The Veil* which was made of fine, twined linen, embroidered in scarlet and purple and blue, and with the cherubim upon it. Into *The Holy of Holies* no one but the High Priest might enter, and he only once a year, on the Day of Atonement, and only after the most elaborate preparations. Within The Holy of Holies stood *The Ark of the Covenant*. It contained three things—the golden pot of the manna, Aaron's rod that budded, and the tables of the law. It was made of acacia wood sheathed outside and lined inside with gold. It was 3 feet 9 inches long, 2 feet 3 inches wide, and 2 feet 3 inches high. Its lid was called *The Mercy Seat*. On The Mercy Seat there were two cherubim of solid gold with overarching wings. It was there that the very presence of God rested, for he had said: "There I will meet with you, and from above the mercy seat, from between the

two cherubim that are upon the ark of the testimony"
(*Exodus* 25: 22).

It was of all this beauty that the writer to the Hebrews
was thinking—and yet it was only a shadow of reality.
In his mind there was another thing of which he was to
speak again—the ordinary Israelite could come only to the
gate of the Tabernacle court; the priests and the Levites
might enter the court; the priests alone might enter the
Holy Place; and none but the High Priest might enter
the Holy of Holies. There was beauty but it was a beauty in
which the common man was barred from the inner presence
of God. Jesus Christ took the barrier away and opened
wide the way to God's presence for every man.

## THE ONLY ENTRY TO THE PRESENCE OF GOD

*Hebrews* 9: 6–10

> Since these preparations have been made, the priests continually
> enter into the first tabernacle as they perform the various acts
> of worship. But into the second tabernacle the High Priest alone
> enters, and that once a year and not without blood, which he
> offers for himself and for the errors of the people. By this the
> Holy Spirit is showing that the way into the Holy Place was not
> yet opened up so long as the first tabernacle stood. Now the
> first tabernacle stands for this present age, and according to its
> services sacrifices are offered which cannot perfect the conscience
> of the worshipper but which, since they are based on food and
> drink and various kinds of washings, are human regulations, laid
> down until the time of the new order should come.

ONLY the High Priest could enter into the Holy of Holies and
that only on *The Day of Atonement*. It is of the ceremonies of
that day that the writer to the Hebrews is here thinking.
He did not need to describe them to his readers for they knew
them. To them they were the most sacred religious ceremonies
in all the world. If we are to understand the thought of the
writer to the Hebrews we must have a picture of them in our
minds. The main description is in *Leviticus* 16.

First, we must ask, what was the idea behind The Day of
Atonement? As we have seen, the relationship between Israel
and God was a covenant relationship. Sin on Israel's part
broke that relationship, and the whole system of sacrifice
existed to make atonement for sin and to restore the broken
relationship. But what if there were some sins still not atoned
for? What if there were some sins of which a man was not
conscious? What if by some chance the altar itself had become
defiled? That is to say, what if the sacrificial system was not
performing the function it should?

The summary of the Day of Atonement is given in
*Leviticus* 16: 33:

> And he shall make atonement for the sanctuary; and he shall
> make atonement for the tent of meeting, and for the altar,
> and he shall make atonement for the priests and for all the
> people of the assembly.

It was one great comprehensive act of atonement for all sin.
It was one grand day in which all things and all people were
cleansed, so that the relationship between Israel and God
should continue unbroken. To that end it was a day of
humiliation. "You shall afflict yourselves" (*Leviticus* 16: 29).
It was not a *feast* but a *fast*. The whole nation fasted all
day, even the boys and girls; and the really devout Jew
prepared himself for it by fasting for the ten days which went
before. The Day of Atonement comes ten days after the
opening of the Jewish New Year, about the beginning of
September in our calendar. It was the greatest of all days
in the life of the High Priest.

Let us then see what happened. Very early in the morning
the High Priest cleansed himself by washing. He donned his
gorgeous robes of office, worn only on that day. There
were the white linen breeches and the long white undergarment
reaching down to the feet, woven in one piece. There was
*The Robe of the Ephod.* It was dark blue and was a long robe
with at the foot a fringe of blue, purple and scarlet tassels
made in the form of pomegranates, interspersed with an equal

number of little golden bells. Over this robe he put *The Ephod* itself. The Ephod was probably a kind of linen tunic, embroidered in scarlet and purple and gold, with an elaborate girdle. On its shoulders were two onyx stones. The names of six of the tribes were engraved on one and six on the other. On the tunic was *The Breastplate*, a span square. On it were twelve precious stones with the names of the twelve tribes engraved upon them. So the High Priest carried the people to God on his shoulders and on his heart. In the breastplate there was the *Urim and the Thummim*, which means *lights and perfections* (*Exodus* 28: 30). What exactly the Urim and the Thummim was is not known. It is known that the High Priest consulted it when he wished to know the will of God. It may be that it was a precious diamond inscribed with the consonants IHWH which are the consonants of *Jahweh*, the name of God. On his head the High Priest put the tall *Mitre,* of fine linen; and on the mitre there was a gold plate bound by a band of blue ribbon, and on the plate were the words: "Holiness unto the Lord." It is easy to imagine what a dazzling figure the High Priest must have presented on this his greatest day.

The High Priest began by doing the things that were done every day. He burned the morning incense, made the morning sacrifice, and attended to the trimming of the lamps on the seven-branched lampstand. Then came the first part of the special ritual of the day. Still dressed in his gorgeous robes, he sacrificed a bullock and seven lambs and one ram (*Numbers* 29: 7). Then he removed his gorgeous robes, cleansed himself again in water, and dressed himself in the simple purity of white linen. There was brought to him a bullock bought with his own resources. He placed his hands on its head and, standing there in the full sight of the people, confessed his own sin and the sin of his house:

> "Ah, Lord God, I have committed iniquity: I have transgressed: I have sinned—I and my house. O Lord, I entreat thee, cover over (atone for) the iniquities, the transgressions, and the sins, which I have committed, transgressed, and sinned before thee, I and my

house, even as it is written in the law of Moses, thy servant, 'For
in that day, he will cover over (atone) for you to make you clean.
From all your transgressions before the Lord you shall be
cleansed.' "

For the moment the bullock was left before the altar. And
then followed one of the unique ceremonies of the Day of
Atonement. Two goats were standing by, and beside the goats
an urn with two lots in it. One lot was marked *For Jehovah*;
the other was marked *For Azazel,* which is the phrase the
Authorized Version translates *The Scapegoat.* The lots were
drawn and laid one on the head of each goat. A tongue-shaped
piece of scarlet was tied to the horn of the scapegoat. And for
the moment the goats were left. Then the High Priest turned
to the bullock which was beside the altar and killed it. Its
throat was slit and the blood caught by a priest in a basin.
The basin was kept in motion so that the blood would not
coagulate for soon it was to be used. Then came the first of the
great moments. The High Priest took coals from the altar and
put them in a censer; he took incense and put it in a special
dish; and then he walked into the Holy of Holies to burn
incense in the very presence of God. It was laid down that he
must not stay too long "lest he put Israel in terror." The people
literally watched with bated breath; and when he came out
from the presence of God still alive, there went up a sigh of
relief like a gust of wind.

When the High Priest came out from the Holy of Holies,
he took the basin of the bullock's blood, went back into the
Holy of Holies and sprinkled it seven times up and seven times
down. He came out, killed the goat that was marked *For
Jehovah,* with its blood re-entered the Holy of Holies and
sprinkled again. Then he came out and mingled together the
blood of the bullock and the goat and seven times sprinkled
the horns of the altar of the incense and the altar itself. What
remained of the blood was laid at the foot of the altar of the
burnt offering. Thus the Holy of Holies and the altar were
cleansed by blood from any defilement that might be on them.

Then came the most vivid ceremony. The scapegoat was

brought forward. The High Priest laid his hands on it and confessed his own sin and the sin of the people; and the goat was led forth into the desert, "into a land not inhabited," laden with the sins of the people and there it was killed.

The priest turned to the slain bullock and goat and prepared them for sacrifice. Still in his linen garments he read scripture—*Leviticus* 16; 23: 27–32, and repeated by heart *Numbers* 29: 7–11. He then prayed for the priesthood and the people. Once again he cleansed himself in water and rearrayed himself in his gorgeous robes. He sacrificed, first, a kid of the goats for the sins of the people; then he made the normal evening sacrifice; then he sacrificed the already prepared parts of the bullock and the goat. Then once again he cleansed himself, took off his robes, and put on the white linen; and for the fourth and last time he entered the Holy of Holies to remove the censer of incense which still burned there. Once again he cleansed himself in water; once again he put on his vivid robes; then he burned the evening offering of incense, trimmed the lamps on the golden lampstand, and his work was done. In the evening he held a feast because he had been in the presence of God and had come out alive.

Such was the ritual of the Day of Atonement, the day designed to cleanse all things and all people from sin. That was the picture in the mind of the writer to the Hebrews and he was to make much of it. But there were certain things of which he was thinking at the moment.

Every year this ceremony had to be gone through again. Everyone but the High Priest was barred from the presence and even he entered in terror. The cleansing was a purely external one by baths of water. The sacrifice was that of bulls and goats and animal blood. The whole thing failed because such things cannot atone for sin. In it all the writer to the Hebrews sees a pale copy of the reality, a ghostly pattern of the one true sacrifice—the sacrifice of Christ. It was a noble ritual, a thing of dignity and beauty; but it was only an unavailing shadow. The only priest and the only sacrifice which can open the way to God for *all* men is Jesus Christ.

## THE SACRIFICE WHICH OPENS THE WAY TO GOD

*Hebrews* 9: 11–14

> But when Christ arrived upon the scene, a high priest of the good
> things which are to come, by means of a tabernacle which was greater
> and better able to produce the results for which it was meant, a
> tabernacle not made by the hands of men—that is, a tabernacle
> which did not belong to this world order—and not by the blood of
> goats and bullocks but by his own blood, he entered once and for
> all into the Holy Place because he had secured for us an eternal
> redemption. For if the blood of goats and bulls and the ashes of a
> heifer could by sprinkling cleanse those that were unclean so that
> their bodies became pure, how much more will the blood of Christ
> who, through the eternal Spirit offered himself spotless to God,
> cleanse your conscience so that you will be able to leave the deeds
> that make for death in order to become the servants of the
> living God?

WHEN we try to understand this passage, we must remember
three things which are basic to the thought of the writer to
the Hebrews. (i) Religion is access to God. Its function is to
bring a man into God's presence. (ii) This is a world of pale
shadows and imperfect copies; beyond is the world of realities.
The function of all worship is to bring men into contact with
the eternal realities. That was what the worship of the
Tabernacle was meant to do; but the earthly Tabernacle and
its worship are pale copies of the real Tabernacle and its
worship; and only the real Tabernacle and the real worship
can give access to reality. (iii) There can be no religion without
sacrifice. Purity is a costly thing; access to God demands
purity; somehow man's sin must be atoned for and his
uncleanness cleansed. With these ideas in his mind the writer
to the Hebrews goes on to show that Jesus is the only High
Priest who brings a sacrifice that can open the way to God and
that that sacrifice is himself.

To begin with, he refers to certain of the great sacrifices
which the Jews were in the habit of making under the old
covenant with God. (i) There was the sacrifice of *bullocks* and

of *goats*. In this he is referring to two of the great sacrifices on The Day of Atonement—of the bullock which the High Priest offered for his own sins and of the scapegoat which was led away to the wilderness bearing the sins of the people (*Leviticus* 16: 15, 21, 22). (ii) There was the sacrifice of the *red heifer*. This strange ritual is described in *Numbers* 19. Under Jewish ceremonial law, if a man touched a dead body, he was unclean. He was barred from the worship of God, and everything and everyone he touched also became unclean. To deal with this there was a prescribed method of cleansing. A red heifer was slaughtered outside the camp. The priest sprinkled the blood of the heifer before the Tabernacle seven times. The body of the beast was then burned, together with cedar and hyssop and a piece of red cloth. The resulting ashes were laid up outside the camp in a clean place and constituted a purification for sin. This ritual must have been very ancient for both its origin and its meaning are wrapped in obscurity. The Jews themselves told that once a Gentile questioned Rabbi Jochanan ben Zakkai on the meaning of this rite, declaring that it sounded like pure superstition. The Rabbi's answer was that it had been appointed by the Holy One and that men must not enquire into his reasons but should leave the matter there without explanation. In any event, the fact remains that it was one of the great rites of the Jews.

The writer to the Hebrews tells of these sacrifices and then declares that the sacrifice that Jesus brings is far greater and far more effective. We must first ask what he means by the greater and more effective tabernacle not made with hands? That is a question to which no one can give an answer which is beyond dispute. But the ancient scholars nearly all took it in one way and said that this new tabernacle which brought men into the very presence of God was nothing else than the body of Jesus. It would be another way of saying what John said: "He who has seen me has seen the Father" (*John* 14: 9). The worship of the ancient tabernacle was designed to bring men into the presence of God. That it could do only in the most shadowy and imperfect way. The coming of Jesus really

brought men into the presence of God, because in him God
entered this world of space and time in a human form and to
see Jesus is to see what God is like.

The great superiority of the sacrifice Jesus brought lay in
three things. (i) The ancient sacrifices cleansed a man's body
from ceremonial uncleanness; the sacrifice of Jesus cleansed
his soul. We must always remember this—in theory all sacrifice
cleansed from transgressions of the ritual law; it did not cleanse
from sins of the presumptuous heart and the high hand. Take
the case of the red heifer. It was not *moral* uncleanness that
its sacrifice wiped out but the ceremonial uncleanness con-
sequent upon touching a dead body. A man's body might be
clean ceremonially and yet his heart be torn with remorse. He
might feel able to enter the tabernacle and yet far away from
the presence of God. The sacrifice of Jesus takes the load of
guilt from a man's *conscience*. The animal sacrifices of the old
covenant might well leave a man in estrangement from God;
the sacrifice of Jesus shows us a God whose arms are always
outstretched and in whose heart is only love.

(ii) The sacrifice of Jesus brought eternal redemption. The
idea was that men were under the dominion of sin; and just
as the purchase price had to be paid to free a man from
slavery, so the purchase price had to be paid to free a man
from sin.

(iii) The sacrifice of Christ enabled a man to leave the deeds
of death and to become the servant of the living God. That
is to say, he did not only win forgiveness for a man's past sin,
he enabled him in the future to live a godly life. The sacrifice
of Jesus was not only the paying of a debt; it was the giving
of a victory. What Jesus did puts a man right with God and
what he does enables a man to stay right with God. The act of
the Cross brings to men the love of God in a way that takes
their terror of him away; the presence of the living Christ
brings to them the power of God so that they can win a daily
victory over sin.

Westcott outlines four ways in which Jesus's sacrifice of
himself differs from the animal sacrifices of the old covenant.

(i) The sacrifice of Jesus was *voluntary*. The animal's life was taken from it; Jesus *gave* his life. He willingly laid it down for his friends.

(ii) The sacrifice of Jesus was *spontaneous*. Animal sacrifice was entirely *the product of law*; the sacrifice of Jesus was entirely *the product of love*. We pay our debts to a tradesman because we have to; we give a gift to our loved ones because we want to. It was not law but love that lay behind the sacrifice of Christ.

(iii) The sacrifice of Jesus was *rational*. The animal victim did not know what was happening; Jesus all the time knew what he was doing. He died, not as an ignorant victim caught up in circumstances over which he had no control and did not understand but with eyes wide open.

(iv) The sacrifice of Jesus was *moral*. Animal sacrifice was mechanical; but Jesus's sacrifice was made, through *the eternal Spirit*. This thing on Calvary was not a matter of prescribed ritual mechanically carried out; it was a matter of Jesus obeying the will of God for the sake of men. Behind it there was not the mechanism of law but the choice of love.

## THE ONLY WAY IN WHICH SINS CAN BE FORGIVEN

*Hebrews* 9: 15–22

It is through him that there emerges a new covenant between God and man; and the purpose behind this new covenant is that those who have been called might receive the eternal inheritance which has been promised to them; but this could happen only after a death had taken place, the purpose of which was to rescue them from the consequences of the transgressions which had been committed under the conditions of the old covenant. For where there is a will, it is necessary that there should be evidence of the death of the testator before the will is valid. It is in the case of dead people that a will is confirmed, since surely it cannot be operative when the testator is still alive. That is why even the first covenant was not

inaugurated without blood. For, after every commandment which
the law lays down had been announced by Moses to all the people,
he took the blood of calves and goats, together with water and scarlet
and hyssop, and sprinkled the book itself and all the people. And as he
did so, he said: "This is the blood of the covenant whose conditions
God commanded you to observe." In like manner he sprinkled with
blood the tabernacle also and all the instruments used in its worship.
Under the conditions which the law lays down it is true to say that
almost everything is cleansed by blood. Without the shedding of
blood there is no forgiveness.

THIS is one of the most difficult passages in the whole letter,
although it would not be difficult to those who read the letter
for the first time, for its methods of argument and expression
and categories of thought would be familiar to them.

As we have seen, the idea of the *covenant* is basic to the
thought of the writer, by which he meant a relationship
between God and man. The first covenant was dependent on
man's keeping of the law; as soon as he broke the law the
covenant became ineffective. Let us remember that to our
writer *religion means access to God.* Therefore, the basic
meaning of the *new covenant,* which Jesus inaugurated, is that
men should have access to God or, to put it another way, have
*fellowship* with him. But here is the difficulty. Men come to the
new covenant already stained with the sins committed under
the old covenant, for which the old sacrificial system was
powerless to atone. So, the writer to the Hebrews has a
tremendous thought and says that the sacrifice of Jesus Christ
is retroactive. That is to say, it is effective to wipe out the sins
of men committed under the old covenant and to inaugurate
the fellowship promised under the new.

All that seems very complicated but at the back of it there
are two great eternal truths. First, the sacrifice of Jesus gains
forgiveness for past sins. We ought to be punished for what
we have done and shut out from God; but because of what
Jesus did the debt is wiped out, the breach is forgiven and the
barrier is taken away. Second, the sacrifice of Jesus opens a
new life for the future. It opens the way to fellowship with God.

The God whom our sins had made a stranger, the sacrifice of Christ has made a friend. Because of what he did the burden of the past is rolled away and life becomes life with God.

It is the next step in the argument which appears to us a fantastic way in which to argue. The question in the mind of the writer is why this new relationship with God should involve the *death* of Christ. He answers it in two ways.

(i) His first answer is—to us almost incredibly—founded on nothing other than a play on words. We have seen that the use of the word *diathēkē* in the sense of *covenant* is characteristically Christian, and that its normal secular use was in the sense of *will* or *testament*. Up to verse 16 the writer to the Hebrews has been using *diathēkē* in the normal Christian sense of *covenant*; then, suddenly and without warning or explanation, he switches to the sense of *will*. Now a *will* does not become operative until the testator dies; so the writer to the Hebrews says that no *diathēkē*, *will*, can be operative until the death of the testator so that the new *diathēkē*, *covenant*, cannot become operative apart from the death of Christ. That is a merely verbal argument and is quite unconvincing to a modern mind; but it must be remembered that this founding of an argument on a play between two meanings of a word was a favourite method of the Alexandrian scholars in the time when this letter was written. In fact this very argument would have been considered in the days when the letter to the Hebrews was written an exceedingly clever piece of exposition.

(ii) His second answer goes back to the Hebrew sacrificial system and to *Leviticus* 17: 11: "The life of the flesh is in the blood; and I have given it for you upon the altar to make atonement for your souls; *for it is the blood that makes atonement*." "Without the shedding of blood there can be no atonement for sin," was actually a well-known Hebrew principle. So the writer to the Hebrews goes back to the inauguration of the first covenant under Moses, the occasion when the people accepted the law as the condition of their special relationship with God. We are told how sacrifice was made and how Moses "took half of the blood and put it in basins; and half of the blood he threw against the altar." After the book of the law had been read and the people had signified their acceptance of it, Moses "took the blood and threw it upon the people, and said, 'Behold the blood of the covenant which the Lord has made with you in accordance with all these words' " (*Exodus* 24: 1–8). It is true that the memory of the writer to the Hebrews of that passage is not strictly accurate. He introduces calves and goats and scarlet and hyssop which come from the ritual of The Day of Atonement and he talks about the sprinkling of the Tabernacle, which at that time had not yet been built; but the reason is that these things are so much in his mind. His basic idea is that there can be no cleansing and no ratification of any covenant without the shedding of blood. *Why* that should be so he does not need to know. Scripture says it is so and that is enough for him. The probable reason is that blood is life, as the Hebrew saw it, and life is the most precious thing in the world; and man must offer his most precious thing to God.

All that goes back to a ritual which is only of antiquarian interest. But behind it there is an eternal principle—*Forgiveness is a costly thing. Human forgiveness* is costly. A son or a daughter may go wrong and a father or a mother may forgive; but that forgiveness brings tears, whiteness to the hair, lines to the face, a cutting anguish and then a long dull ache to the heart. It does not cost nothing. *Divine forgiveness* is costly. God is love but he is also *holiness*. He least of all can break the great moral laws on which the universe is built. Sin must have its punishment or the very structure of life disintegrates. And God alone can pay the terrible price that is necessary before men can be forgiven. Forgiveness is never a case of saying: "It's all right; it doesn't matter." It is the most costly thing in the world. Without the shedding of heart's blood there can be no forgiveness of sins. Nothing brings a man to his senses with such arresting violence as to see the effect of his sin on someone who loves him in this world or on the God who loves him for ever, and to say to himself: "It cost *that* to forgive *my* sin." Where there is forgiveness someone must be crucified.

## THE PERFECT PURIFICATION

*Hebrews* 9: 23–28

So, then, if it was necessary that the things which are copies of the heavenly realities should be cleansed by processes like these, it is necessary that the heavenly realities themselves should be cleansed by finer sacrifices than those of which we have been thinking. It is not into a man-made sanctuary that Christ has entered—that would be a mere symbol of the things which are real. It is into heaven itself that he entered, now to appear on our behalf before the presence of God. It is not that he has to offer himself repeatedly, as the High Priest year by year enters into the Holy Place with a blood that is not his own. Were that so he would have had to suffer again and again since the world was founded. But now, as things are, once and for all, at the end of the ages, he has appeared with his sacrifice of himself so that our sins should be cancelled. And just as it is laid down for men to die once and for all and then to face the judgment, so Christ, after being once and for all sacrificed to bear the burden of the sins of many, will appear a second time, not this time to deal with sin, but for the salvation of those who are waiting for him.

THE writer to the Hebrews, still thinking of the supreme efficacy of the sacrifice which Jesus made, begins with a flight of thought which, even for so adventurous a writer as he, is amazing. Let us remember again the letter's basic thought that the worship of this world is a pale copy of the real worship. The writer to the Hebrews says that in this world the Levitical sacrifices were designed to purify the means of worship. For instance, the sacrifices of the Day of Atonement purified the tabernacle and the altar and the Holy Place. Now he goes on to say that the work of Christ purifies *not only earth but heaven*. He has the tremendous thought of a kind of cosmic redemption that purified the whole universe, seen and unseen.

So he goes on to stress again the way in which the work and the sacrifice of Christ are supreme.

(i) Christ entered into no man-made Holy Place; he entered into the presence of God. We are to think of Christianity not in terms of Church membership but in terms of intimate fellowship with God.

(ii) Christ entered into the presence of God not only for his own sake but for ours. It was to open the way for us and plead our cause. In Christ there is the greatest paradox in the world, the paradox of the greatest glory and the greatest service, the paradox of one for whom the world exists and who exists for the world, the paradox of the eternal King and the eternal Servant.

(iii) The sacrifice of Christ never needs to be made again. Year after year the ritual of the Day of Atonement had to go on and the things that blocked the road to God had to be atoned for; but through Christ's sacrifice the road to God is for ever open. Men were always sinners and always will be but that does not mean that Christ must go on offering himself again and again. The road is open once and for all. We can have a faint analogy of that. For long a certain surgical operation may be impossible. Then some surgeon finds a way round the difficulties. From that day that same road is open to all surgeons. We may put it this way—nothing need ever be added to what Jesus Christ has done to keep open the way to God's love for sinning men.

Finally, the writer to the Hebrews draws a parallel between the life of man and the life of Christ.

(i) Man dies and then comes the judgment. That itself was a shock to the Greek for he tended to believe that death was final. "When earth once drinks the blood of a man," said Aeschylus, "there is death once and for all and there is no resurrection." Euripides says: "It cannot be the dead to light shall come." "For the one loss is this that never mortal maketh good again the life of man—though wealth may be re-won." Homer makes Achilles say when he reaches the shades: "Rather would I live upon the soil as the hireling of another, with a landless man whose livelihood was small, than bear sway among all the dead who are no more." Mimnermus writes with a kind of despair:

> "O Golden love, what life, what joy but thine?
> Come death, when thou art gone, and make an end!"

There is a simple Greek epitaph:

> "Farewell, tomb of Melitē; the best of women lies here, who loved her loving husband, Onesimus; thou wert most excellent, wherefore he longs for thee after thy death, for thou wert the best of wives. Farewell thou too, dearest husband, only love my children."

As G. Lowes Dickinson points out, in the Greek, the first and the last word of that epitaph is "Farewell!" Death was the end. When Tacitus is writing the tribute of biography to the great Agricola all he can finish with is an "if."

> "If there be any habitation for the spirits of just men, if, as the sages will have it, great souls perish not with the body, mayest thou rest in peace."

"If" is the only word. Marcus Aurelius can say that when a man dies and his spark goes back to be lost in God, all that is left is "dust, ashes, bones, and stench." The significant thing about this passage of Hebrews is its basic assumption that a man will rise again. That is part of the certainty of the Christian creed; and the basic warning is that he rises to judgment.

(ii) With Christ it is different—he dies and rises and comes again, and he comes not to be judged but to judge. The early Church never forgot the hope of the Second Coming. It throbbed through their belief. But for the unbeliever that was a day of terror. As *Enoch* had it of the Day of the Lord, before Christ came: "For all you who are sinners there is no salvation, but upon you all will come destruction and a curse." In some way the consummation must come. If in that day Christ comes as a friend, it can be only a day of glory; if he comes as a stranger or as one whom we have regarded as an enemy, it can be only a day of judgment. A man may look to the end of things with joyous expectation or with shuddering terror. What makes the difference is how his heart is with Christ.

## THE ONLY TRUE SACRIFICE

*Hebrews* 10: 1–10

> Because the law is only a pale shadow of the blessings which
> are to come and not a real image of these things, it can never
> really fit for the fellowship of God those who seek to draw
> near to his presence with the sacrifices which have to be brought
> year by year and which go on for ever. For if these sacrifices
> could achieve that, would they not have stopped being brought
> because the worshipper had been once and for all brought
> into a state of purity and no longer had any consciousness of
> sin? So far from that, in them there is a year by year reminder
> of sin. For it is impossible for the blood of bulls and goats to
> take away sin. That is why he says as he enters the world: "You
> did not desire sacrifice and offering; it is a body you have
> prepared for me. You took no pleasure in whole burnt-offerings
> and in sin-offerings. So then I said: 'So then I come—in the roll
> of the book it is written of me—to do, O God, your will.'" At the
> beginning of this passage he says: "You did not desire sacrifices
> and offerings and whole burnt-offerings and sin-offerings and you
> took no pleasure in them," and it is such offerings as these that
> the law prescribes. Then he went on to say: "Behold, I come to do
> your will." He abolishes the kind of offerings referred to in the
> first quotation in order to establish the kind of offering referred
> to in the second. It is by this way of "the will" that we have been
> purified through the once and for all offering of the body of Christ.

To the writer to the Hebrews the whole business of sacrifice
was only a pale copy of what real worship ought to be. The
business of religion was to bring a man into a close
relationship with God and that is what these sacrifices
could never do. The best that they could do was to give him
a distant and spasmodic contact with God. He uses two
words to indicate what he means. He says that these things
are a *pale shadow*. The word he uses is *skia*, the Greek for *a
shadow*, and it means a nebulous reflection, a mere silhouette,
a form without reality. He says that they do not give a *real
image*. The word he uses is *eikōn,* which means a *complete
representation, a detailed reproduction.* It actually does mean a

*portrait,* and would mean a *photograph,* if there had been such a thing in those days. In effect he is saying: "Without Christ you cannot get beyond the shadows of God."

He brings proof. Year by year the sacrifices of the Tabernacle and especially of the Day of Atonement go on. An effective thing does not need to be done again; the very fact of the repetition of these sacrifices is the final proof that they are *not* purifying men's souls and *not* giving full and uninterrupted access to God. Our writer goes further—he says that all they are is *a reminder of sin.* So far from purifying a man, they remind him that he is not purified and that his sins still stand between him and God.

Let us take an analogy. A man is ill. A bottle of medicine is prescribed for him. If that medicine effects a cure, every time he looks at the bottle thereafter, he will say: "That is what gave me back my health." On the other hand, if the medicine is ineffective, every time he looks at the bottle he will be reminded that he is ill and that the recommended cure was useless.

So the writer to the Hebrews says with prophetic vehemence: "The sacrifice of animals is powerless to purify a man and give him access to God. All that such sacrifices can do is to remind a man that he is an uncured sinner and that the barrier of his sin is between himself and God." So far from erasing his sin, they underline it.

The only effective sacrifice is the sacrifice of Jesus Christ. To make his point and to explain what is in his mind, Hebrews takes a quotation from *Psalm* 40: 6–9. In the Revised Standard Version, which is close to the original Hebrew, the passage runs:

> "Sacrifice and offering thou dost not desire;
> but thou hast given me an open ear.
> Burnt-offering and sin-offering thou hast not required.
> Then I said: Lo I come;
> In the roll of the book it is written of me.
> I delight to do thy will, O my God."

The writer to the Hebrews quotes it differently and in the second line he has:

"A body you have prepared for me."

The explanation is that he was not quoting from the original Hebrew but from the Septuagint, the Greek translation of the Old Testament. About 270 B.C. the task of translating the Old Testament into Greek was begun in Alexandria in Egypt. Obviously far more people in the ancient world read Greek than Hebrew. It is very likely that the writer to the Hebrews did not know any Hebrew at all and therefore it is the Septuagint that he uses. In any event the meaning of the two phrases is the same. "Thou hast given me an open ear," means, "You have so touched me that everything I hear I obey." It is the obedient ear of which the psalmist is thinking. "A body you have prepared for me," really means, "You created me that in my body and with my body I should do your will." In essence the meaning is the same.

The writer to the Hebrews has taken the words of the psalm and put them into the mouth of Jesus. What they say is that God wants not animal sacrifices but *obedience to his will*. In its essence sacrifice was a noble thing. It meant that a man was taking something dear to him and giving it to God to show his love. But human nature being what it is it was easy for the idea to degenerate and for sacrifice to be thought of as a way of buying God's forgiveness.

The writer to the Hebrews was not saying anything new when he said that obedience was the only true sacrifice. Long before him the prophets had seen how sacrifice had degenerated and had told the people that what God wanted was not the blood and the flesh of animals but the obedience of a man's life. That is precisely one of the noblest thoughts of the Old Testament men of God.

"And Samuel said, has the Lord as great delight in burnt-offerings and sacrifices, as in obeying the voice of the Lord? Behold, to obey is better than sacrifice, and to hearken than the fat of rams" (1 *Samuel* 15: 22).

"Offer to God a sacrifice of thanksgiving; and pay your vows to the Most High" (*Psalm* 50: 14).

"For thou hast no delight in sacrifice; were I to give a burnt offering, thou wouldst not be pleased. The sacrifice acceptable to God is a broken spirit; a broken and contrite heart, O God, thou wilt not despise." (*Psalm* 51: 16, 17).

"For I desire steadfast love and not sacrifice, the knowledge of God, rather than burnt offerings." (*Hosea* 6: 6).

"What to me is the multitude of your sacrifices? says the Lord; I have had enough of burnt offerings of rams and the fat of fed beasts; I do not delight in the blood of bulls, or of lambs, or of he-goats. . . . Bring no more vain offerings; incense is an abomination to me. . . . When you spread forth your hands, I will hide my eyes from you; even though you make many prayers, I will not listen; your hands are full of blood. . . . Cease to do evil, learn to do good" (*Isaiah* 1: 11–20).

"With what shall I come before the Lord, and bow myself before God on high? Shall I come before him with burnt offerings, with calves a year old? Will the Lord be pleased with thousands of rams, with ten thousands of rivers of oil? Shall I give my first-born for my transgression, the fruit of my body for the sin of my soul?" He has showed you, O man, what is good; and what does the Lord require of you but to do justice, and to love kindness, and to walk humbly with your God." (*Micah* 6: 6–8).

Always there had been voices crying out for God that the only sacrifice was that of obedience. Nothing but obedience could open the way to God; disobedience set up a barrier that no animal sacrifice could ever take away. Jesus was the perfect sacrifice *because he perfectly did God's will.* He took himself and said to God: "Do with me as you will." He brought to God for men what no man had been able to bring— the perfect obedience, that was the perfect sacrifice.

If we are ever to have fellowship with God, obedience is the only way. What man could not offer, Jesus offered. In his perfect manhood he offered the perfect sacrifice of the perfect obedience. Through that the way was once and for all opened up for us.

## THE FINALITY OF CHRIST

*Hebrews* 10: 11–18

> Again, every priest stands every day engaged upon his service;
> he stands offering the same sacrifices over and over again, and
> they are sacrifices of such a kind that they can never take away
> sins. But he offered one single sacrifice for sin and then took his
> seat for ever at the right hand of God, and for the future he waits
> until his enemies are made the footstool of his feet. For by one
> offering and for all time he perfectly gave us that cleansing we
> need to enter into the presence of God. And to this the Holy Spirit
> is our witness, for after he has said: "This is the covenant I will
> make with them after these days, says the Lord. I will put my
> laws upon their hearts; and I will write them upon their minds,"
> he goes on to say. "And I will not remember any more their sins
> and their breaches of the law." Now, where there is forgiveness
> of these things, a sacrifice for sin is no longer necessary.

ONCE again the writer to the Hebrews is drawing a series of
implicit contrasts between the sacrifice that Jesus offered
and the animal sacrifices that the priests offer.

(i) He stresses *the achievement of Jesus.* The sacrifice of
Jesus was made once and is effective for ever; the animal
sacrifices of the priests must be made over and over again,
and even then they are not effective in any real way. Every
day, so long as the Temple stood, the following sacrifices had
to be carried out (*Numbers* 28: 3–8). Every morning and
every evening a male lamb of one year old, without spot and
blemish, was offered as a *burnt-offering.* Along with it there
was offered a *meat-offering,* which consisted of one tenth
of an ephah of fine flour mixed with a quarter of a hin of pure
oil. There was also a *drink-offering*, which consisted of a
quarter of a hin of wine. Added to that there was *the daily
meat-offering of the High Priest*; it consisted of one-tenth of an
ephah of fine flour, mixed with oil, and baked in a flat pan;
half was offered in the morning and half in the evening. In
addition there was an offering of *incense* before these offerings
in the morning and after them in the evening. There was a kind

of priestly tread-mill of sacrifice. Moffatt speaks of "the
levitical drudges" who, day in day out, kept offering these
sacrifices. There was no end to this process and it left men still
conscious of their sin and alienated from God.

In contrast, Jesus had made a sacrifice that neither could
nor need be repeated.

(*a*) It *could* not be repeated. There is something unrepeatable
about any great work. It is possible to repeat the popular tunes
of the day *ad infinitum*; to a great extent one echoes another.
But it is not possible to repeat the Fifth or the Ninth
Symphony of Beethoven; no one else will ever write anything
like them. It is possible to repeat the kind of poetry that is
written in sentimental journals and on Christmas cards; but
not to repeat the blank verse of Shakespeare's plays or the
hexametres of Homer's *Iliad*. These things stand alone.
Certain things can be repeated; but all works of genius have
a certain unrepeatable quality. It is so with the sacrifice of
Christ. It is *sui generis*; it is one of these masterpieces which
can never be done again.

(*b*) It *need* not be repeated. For one thing, *the sacrifice of
Jesus perfectly shows the love of God*. In that life of service
and in that death of love, there stands fully displayed the
heart of God. Looking at Jesus, we can say: "That is what
God is like." For another thing, *the life and death of Jesus
was an act of perfect obedience and, therefore, the only
perfect sacrifice*. All scripture, at its deepest, declares that the
only sacrifice God desires is obedience; and in the life and
death of Jesus that is precisely the sacrifice that God received.
Perfection cannot be improved upon. In Jesus there is at one
and the same time the perfect revelation of God and the
perfect offering of obedience. Therefore his sacrifice cannot
and need not ever be made again. The priests must go on
with their weary routine of animal sacrifice; but the sacrifice
of Christ was made once and for all.

(ii) He stresses *the exaltation of Jesus*. It is with care that
he picks his words. The priests *stand* offering sacrifice; Christ
*sits* at the right hand of God. Theirs is the position of a

servant; his is the position of a monarch. Jesus is the King come home, his task accomplished and his victory won. There is a *wholeness* about the life of Jesus that perhaps we ought to give more thought. His life is incomplete without his death; his death is incomplete without his resurrection; his resurrection is incomplete without his return to glory. It is the same Jesus who lived and died and rose again and is at the right hand of God. He is not simply a saint who lived a lovely life; not simply a martyr who died an heroic death; not simply a risen figure who returned to company with his friends. He is the Lord of glory. His life is like a panelled tapestry; to look at one panel is to see only a little bit of the story. The tapestry must be looked on as a whole before the full greatness is disclosed.

(iii) He stresses *the final triumph of Jesus*. He awaits the final subjugation of his enemies; in the end there must come a universe in which he is supreme. How that will come is not ours to know; but it may be that this final subjugation will consist not in the extinction of his enemies but in their submission to his love. It is not so much the power but the love of God which must conquer in the end.

Finally, as is his habit, the writer to the Hebrews clinches his argument with a quotation from scripture. Jeremiah, speaking of the new covenant which will not be imposed on a man from outside but which will be written on his heart, ends: "I will remember their sin no more" (*Jeremiah* 31: 34). Because of Jesus the barrier of sin is for ever taken away.

## THE MEANING OF CHRIST FOR US

*Hebrews* 10: 19–25

Since then, brothers, in virtue of what the blood of Jesus has done for us, we can confidently enter into the Holy Place by the new and living way which Jesus inaugurated for us through the veil— that is, through his flesh—and since we have a great High Priest who is over the house of God, let us approach the presence of God

with a heart wherein the truth dwells and with the full conviction
of faith, with our hearts so sprinkled that they are cleansed from
all consciousness of evil and with our bodies washed with pure
water. Let us hold fast to the undeviating hope of our creed,
for we can rely absolutely on him who made the promises;
and let us put our minds to the task of spurring each other on in
love and fine deeds. Let us not abandon our meeting together—
as some habitually do—but let us encourage one another, and
all the more so as we see the Day approaching.

THE writer to the Hebrews now comes to the practical
implication of all that he has been saying. From theology
he turns to practical exhortation. He is one of the deepest
theologians in the New Testament but all his theology is
governed by the pastoral instinct. He does not think merely for
the thrill of intellectual satisfaction but only that he may the
more forcibly appeal to men to enter into the presence of God.

He begins by saying three things about Jesus.

(i) *Jesus is the living way to the presence of God.* We
enter into the presence of God by means of the veil, that is,
by the flesh of Jesus. That is a difficult thought, but what he
means is this. Before the Holy of Holies in the Tabernacle
hung the veil to screen off the presence of God. For men
to enter into that presence the veil would have to be torn
apart. Jesus's flesh is what veiled his godhead. Charles Wesley
in his great hymn appealed to men:

> "Veiled in flesh the godhead see."

It was when the flesh of Christ was rent upon the Cross that
men really saw God. All his life showed God; but it was on the
Cross that God's love really was revealed. As the rending of
the Tabernacle veil opened the way to the presence of God, so
the rending of the flesh of Christ revealed the full greatness of
his love and opened up the way to him.

(ii) *Jesus is the High Priest over God's house in the heavens.*
As we have seen so often, the function of the priest was to
build a bridge between man and God. This means that Jesus
not only shows us the way to God but also when we get there

introduces us to his very presence. A man might be able to direct an enquirer to Buckingham Palace and yet be very far from having the right to take him into the presence of the Queen; but Jesus can take us the whole way.

(iii) *Jesus is the one person who can really cleanse.* In the priestly ritual, the holy things were cleansed by being sprinkled with the blood of the sacrifices. Again and again the High Priest bathed himself in the laver of clear water. But these things were ineffective to remove the real pollution of sin. Only Jesus can really cleanse a man. His is no external purification; by his presence and his Spirit he cleanses the inmost thoughts and desires of a man until he is really clean.

From this the writer to the Hebrews goes on to urge three things.

(i) *Let us approach the presence of God.* That is to say, let us never forget the duty of worship. It is given to every man to live in two worlds, this world of space and time, and the world of eternal things. Our danger is that to become so involved in this world that we forget the other. As the day begins, as the day ends and ever and again in the midst of its activities, we should turn aside, if only for a moment, and enter God's presence. Every man carries with him his own secret shrine, but so many forget to enter it. As Matthew Arnold wrote:

> "But each day brings its pretty dust
> Our soon-choked souls to fill;
> And we forget because we must,
> And not because we will."

(ii) *Let us hold fast to our creed.* That is to say, let us never lose our grip of what we believe. The cynical voices may try to take our faith away; the materialist and his arguments may try to make us forget God; the events of life may conspire to shake our faith. Stevenson said that he so believed in the ultimate decency of things that if he woke up in hell he would still believe in it; and we must have a grip on the faith that nothing can loosen.

(iii) *Let us put our minds to the task of taking thought for others*. That is to say, let us remember that we are Christians not only for our own sake but also for the sake of others. No man ever saved his soul who devoted his whole time and energy to saving it; but many a man has saved it by being so concerned for others that he forgot that he himself had a soul to save. It is easy to drift into a kind of selfish Christianity; but a selfish Christianity is a contradiction in terms.

But the writer to the Hebrews goes on to outline our duty to others in the most practical way. He sees that duty extend in three directions.

(i) *We must spur each other to noble living*. Best of all we can do that by setting the fine example. We can do it by reminding others of their traditions, their privileges, their responsibilities when they are likely to forget them. It has been said that a saint is someone in whom Christ stands revealed; we can seek ever to incite others to goodness by showing them Christ. We may remember how the dying soldier lad looked up at Florence Nightingale and murmured: "You're Christ to me."

(ii) *We must worship together*. There were some amongst those to whom the writer of the Hebrews was writing who had abandoned the habit of meeting together. It is still possible for a man to think that he is a Christian and yet abandon the habit of worshipping with God's people in God's house on God's day. He may try to be what Moffatt called "a pious particle," a Christian in isolation. Moffatt distinguishes three reasons which keep a man from worshipping with his fellow Christians.

(*a*) He may not go to church because of *fear*. He may be ashamed to be seen going to church. He may live or work among people who laugh at those who do so. He may have friends who have no use for that kind of thing and may fear their criticism and contempt. He may, therefore, try to be a secret disciple; but it has been well said that this is impossible because either "the discipleship kills the secrecy or the secrecy kills the discipleship." It would be well if we remembered that, apart from anything else, to go to church is to demonstrate where our loyalty lies. Even if the sermon be poor and the worship tawdry, the church service still gives us the chance to show to men what side we are on.

(*b*) He may not go because of *fastidiousness*. He may shrink from contact with people who are "not like himself." There are congregations which are as much clubs as they are churches. They may be in neighbourhoods where the social status has come down; and the members who have remained faithful to them would be as much embarrassed as delighted if the poor people in the area came flooding in. We must never forget that there is no such thing as a "common" man in the sight of God. It was for *all* men, not only for the respectable classes, that Christ died.

(*c*) He may not go because of *conceit*. He may believe that he does not need the Church or that he is intellectually beyond the standard of preaching there. Social snobbery is bad but spiritual and intellectual snobbery is worse. The wisest man is a fool in the sight of God; and the strongest man is weak in the moment of temptation. There is no man who can live the Christian life and neglect the fellowship of the Church. If any man feels that he can do so let him remember that he comes to Church not only *to get* but *to give*. If he thinks that the Church has faults, it is his duty to come in and help to mend them.

(iii) *We must encourage one another*. One of the highest of human duties is that of encouragement. There is a regulation of the Royal Navy which says: "No officer shall speak discouragingly to another officer in the discharge of his duties." Eliphaz unwillingly paid Job a great tribute. As Moffatt translates it: "Your words have kept men on their feet" (*Job* 4: 4). Barrie somewhere wrote to Cynthia Asquith: "Your first instinct is always to telegraph to Jones the nice thing Brown said about him to Robinson. You have sown a lot of happiness that way." It is easy to laugh at men's ideals, to pour cold water on their enthusiasm, to discourage them. The world is full of discouragers; we have a Christian duty to encourage one another. Many a time a word of praise or thanks or appreciation or cheer has kept a man on his feet. Blessed is the man who speaks such a word.

Finally, the writer to the Hebrews says that our Christian duty to each other is all the more pressing because the time is short. The Day is approaching. He is thinking of the Second Coming of Christ when things as we know them will be ended. The early Church lived in that expectation. Whether or not we still do, we must realize that no man knows when the summons to rise and go will come to him also. In the time we have it is our duty to do all the good we can to all the people we can in all the ways we can.

## THE THREAT AT THE HEART OF THINGS

*Hebrews* 10: 26–31

> For, if we deliberately sin after we have received full knowledge of the truth, no sacrifice for sin is left. All that we can expect is to wait in terror for judgment and for that flaming wrath which will consume the adversaries of God. Anyone who regards the law of Moses as a dead letter dies without pity on the evidence of two or three witnesses. Of how much worse punishment, do you think, that man will be deemed worthy who has trampled underfoot the Son of God, who has failed to regard the blood of the new covenant, with which he was made fit for God's presence, as a sacred thing, and who has insulted the Spirit through whom God's grace comes to us? For we know who it was who said: "Vengeance belongs to me; it is I who will repay," and again: "The Lord will judge his people." It is a terrifying thing to fall into the hands of the living God.

EVERY now and again the writer to the Hebrews speaks with a sternness that is almost without parallel in the New Testament. Few writers have such a sense of the sheer horror of sin. In this passage his thoughts are going back to the grim instruction in *Deuteronomy* 17: 2–7. It is there laid down that, if any person shall be proved to have gone after strange gods and to have worshipped them, "you shall bring forth to your gates that man or woman who has done this evil thing, and you shall stone that man or woman to death with stones. On the evidence of two witnesses or of three witnesses he that is to die shall be put to death; a person shall not be put to death on the evidence of one witness. The hand of the witnesses shall be first against him to put him to death, and afterward the hand of all the people. So you shall purge the evil from the midst of you."

The writer to the Hebrews has this horror of sin for two reasons.

First, he lived in a day when the Church had been under attack and would be under attack again. Its greatest peril was from the possible evil living and apostasy of its members. A Church in such circumstances could not afford to carry members who were a bad advertisement for the Christian faith. Its members must be loyal or nothing. That is still true. Dick Sheppard spent much of his life preaching in the open air to people who were either hostile or indifferent to the Church. From their questions and their arguments and their criticisms he said that he had learned that "the greatest handicap the Church has is the unsatisfactory lives of professing Christians." The unsatisfactory Christian undermines the very foundations of the Church.

Second, he was sure that sin had become doubly serious because of the new knowledge of God and of God's will which Jesus had brought. One of the old divines wrote a kind of catechism. He ends by asking what happens if men disregard the offer of Jesus Christ. His answer is that condemnation must necessarily follow, "and so much the more *because thou hast read this book.*" The greater the knowledge, the greater the sin. The conviction of the writer to the Hebrews was that, if under the old law, apostasy was a terrible thing, it had become doubly terrible now that Christ had come.

He gives us three definitions of sin.

(i) *Sin is to trample Christ under foot.* It is not mere rebelliousness against law; it is the wounding of love. A man can stand almost any attack on his body; the thing that beats him is a broken heart. It is told that in the days of the Hitler terror there was a man in Germany who was arrested, tried, tortured and put into a concentration camp. He faced it all with gallantry and emerged erect and unbroken. Then by accident he discovered who it was who had laid information against him—it was his own son. The discovery broke him and he died. Attack by an enemy he could bear; attack by one whom he loved killed him. When Caesar was murdered he faced his assassins with almost disdainful courage. But when he saw the hand of his friend Brutus raised to strike, he wrapped his head in his mantle and died. Once Christ had come, the awfulness of sin lay not in its breaking of the law but in its trampling of the love of Christ under foot.

(ii) *Sin is the failure to see the sacredness of sacred things.* Nothing produces a shudder like sacrilege. The writer to the Hebrews says in effect: "Look at what has been done for you; look at the shed blood and the broken body of Christ; look at what your new relationship to God cost; can you treat it as if it did not matter? Don't you see what a sacred thing it is?" Sin is the failure to realize the sacredness of that sacrifice upon the Cross.

(iii) *Sin is the insult to the Holy Spirit.* The Holy Spirit speaks within us, telling us what is right and wrong, seeking to check us when we are on the way to sin and to spur us on when we are drifting into lethargy. To disregard these voices is to insult the Spirit and to grieve the heart of God.

All through this, one thing comes out. Sin is not disobedience to an impersonal law; it is the wrecking of a personal relationship and the wounding of the heart of the God whose name is Father.

The writer to the Hebrews finishes his appeal with a threat. He quotes *Deuteronomy* 32: 35, 36 where the sternness of God is clearly seen. At the heart of Christianity there remains for ever a threat. To remove that threat is to emasculate the faith. At the end of the day it is not all one for the good and the bad man alike. No man can evade the fact that in the end judgment comes.


## THE DANGER OF DRIFT

*Hebrews* 10: 32–39

> Remember the former days. Remember how, after you had been enlightened, you had to go through a hard struggle of suffering, partly because you yourselves were held up to insult and involved in affliction and partly because you had become partners with people whose life was like that. For you gave your sympathy to those in prison; you accepted the pillaging of your goods with joy; for you knew that you yourselves hold a possession which is better and which lasts. Do not throw away your confidence, for it is a confidence that has a great reward. You need fortitude so that, after you have done the will of God, you may receive the promise. For in a short time, a very short time, "He who is to come will come and he will not delay. And my just man shall live by faith; but if he shrinks back, my soul will not find pleasure in him." We are not men to shrink back from things and so to come to disaster, but we are men of a faith which will enable us to possess our souls.

THERE had been a time when those to whom this letter was written had been up against it. When first they had become Christians they had known persecution and plundering of their goods; and they had learned what it was to become involved with those under suspicion and unpopular. They had met that situation with gallantry and with honour; and now, when they were in danger of drifting away, the writer to the Hebrews reminds them of their former loyalty.

It is a truth of life that in many ways it is easier to stand adversity than to stand prosperity. Ease has ruined far more men than trouble ever did. The classic example is what happened to the armies of Hannibal.

Hannibal of Carthage was the one general who had routed

the Roman legions. But winter came and the campaign had to be suspended. Hannibal wintered his troops in Capua which he had captured, a city of luxury. And one winter in Capua did what the Roman legions had not succeeded in doing. The luxury so sapped the morale of the Carthaginian troops that when the spring came and the campaign was resumed they were unable to stand before the Romans.

Ease had ruined them when struggle had only toughened them. That is often true of Christian life. Often a man can meet with honour the great hour of testing and of trial; and yet lets the time of plain sailing sap his strength and emasculate his faith.

The appeal of the writer to the Hebrews is one that could be made to every man. In effect, he says: "Be what you were at your best." If only we were always at our best, life would be very different. Christianity does not demand the impossible; but if we were always as honest, as kind, as courageous, as courteous as we can be, life would be transformed.

To be such we need certain things.

(i) *We need to keep our hope before us*. The athlete will make his great effort because the goal beckons him on. He will submit to the discipline of training because of the end in view. If life is only a day to day doing of the routine things, we may well sink into a policy of drift; but if we are on the way to heaven's crown, effort must always be at full pitch.

(ii) *We need fortitude*. Perseverance is one of the great unromantic virtues. Most people can start well and almost everyone can be fine in spasms. To everyone it is sometimes given to mount up with wings as eagles; in the moment of the great effort everyone can run and not be weary; but the greatest gift of all is to walk and not to faint.

(iii) *We need the memory of the end*. The writer to the Hebrews makes a quotation from *Habbakuk* 2: 3. The prophet tells his people that if they hold fast to their loyalty, God will see them through their present situation. The victory comes only to the man who holds on.

To the writer to the Hebrews life was a thing that was on

its way to the presence of Christ. It was therefore never something that could be allowed to drift; it was its end which made the process of life all important, and only the man who endured to the end would be saved.

Here is a summons never to be less than our best; and always to remember that the end comes. If life is the road to Christ none can afford to miss it or to stop half-way.

## THE CHRISTIAN HOPE

*Hebrews* 11: 1–3

> Faith means that we are certain of the things we hope for, convinced of the thing we do not see. It was because of faith that the men of old time had their record attested. It is by faith that we understand that the world was fashioned by the word of God, so that what is seen came into being out of what is unseen.

To the writer to the Hebrews faith is absolutely certain that what it believes is true and that what it expects will come. It is not the hope which looks forward with wistful longing; it is the hope which looks forward with utter conviction. In the early days of persecution they brought a humble Christian before the judges. He told them that nothing they could do could shake him because he believed that, if he was true to God, God would be true to him. "Do you really think," asked the judge, "that the like of you will go to God and his glory?" "I do not think," said the man, "I know." At one time Bunyan was tortured by uncertainty. "Everyone doth think his own Religion rightest," he said, "both Jews and Moors and Pagans; and how if all our Faith and Christ and Scriptures should be but a 'Think so' too?" But when the light broke he ran out crying, "Now I know! I know!" The Christian faith is a hope that has turned to certainty.

This Christian hope is such that it dictates all a man's conduct. He lives in it and he dies in it; and it is the possession of it which makes him act as he does.

As Silesius sang:

"With Hope for pilgrim's staff I go,
    And Patience is my travelling dress
Wherewith through earthly weal and woe,
    I fare to everlastingness."

Moffatt distinguishes three directions in which the Christian hope operates.

(i) It is *belief in God against the world.* If we follow the world's standards we may well have ease and comfort and prosperity; if we follow God's standards we may well have pain and loss and unpopularity. It is the conviction of the Christian that it is better to suffer with God than to prosper with the world. In the book of *Daniel,* Shadrach, Meshach and Abed-nego are confronted with the choice of obeying Nebuchadnezzar and worshipping the king's image or obeying God and entering the fiery furnace. Without hesitation they choose God (*Daniel* 3). When Bunyan was due for trial he said: "With God's comfort in my poor soul, before I went down to the justices I begged of God that if I might do more good by being at liberty than in prison, then I might be set at liberty. But if not, his will be done." The Christian attitude is that in terms of eternity it is better to stake everything on God than to trust to the rewards of the world.

(ii) The Christian hope is *belief in the spirit against the senses.* The senses say to a man: "Take what you can touch and taste and handle and enjoy."

"Gather ye rosebuds while ye may,
    Old Time is still a-flying;
And this same flower that smiles today
    Tomorrow will be dying."

The senses tell us to grasp the thing of the moment; the spirit tells us that there is something far beyond that. The Christian believes in the spirit rather than the senses.

(iii) The Christian hope is *belief in the future against the present.* Long ago Epicurus said the chief end of life was pleasure. But he did not mean what so many people think he meant. He insisted that we must take the long view. The thing which is pleasant at the moment may bring pain in the long run; the thing which hurts like fury at the moment may bring joy in the long run. The Christian is certain that in the long run no man can exile the truth for "great is truth, and in the end she will prevail."

It looked as if his judges had eliminated Socrates and as if Pilate had crushed Christ; but the verdict of the future reversed the verdict of the moment. Fosdick somewhere says that Nero once condemned Paul, but the years have passed on and the time has come when men call their sons Paul and their dogs Nero.

It is easy to argue: "Why should I refuse the pleasure of the moment for an uncertain future?" The Christian answer is that the future is *not* uncertain because it belongs to God; and it is enough that God has commanded and that God has promised.

The writer to the Hebrews goes on to say that it was precisely because the great heroes of the faith lived on that principle that they were approved by God. Every one of them refused what the world calls greatness and staked everything on God— and history proved them right.

The writer to the Hebrews goes further. He says that it is an act of faith to believe that God made this world and adds that the things which are seen emerged from the things which are not seen. This was aiming a blow at the current belief that God created the world out of existing matter which, being necessarily imperfect, meant that from the beginning this was an imperfect world. The writer to the Hebrews insists that God did not work with existing material but created the world from nothing. When he argued like this he was not interested in the scientific side of the matter, he wanted to stress the fact that *this is God's world.*

If we can grip that fact, two things follow. First, we will use it as such. We will remember that everything in it is God's and will try to use it as God would have us use it. Second, we will remember that, even when it may not look like it, somehow God is in control. If we believe that this is God's world

then into our lives come a new sense of responsibility and a
new power of acceptance, for everything belongs to God and
all is in his hands.

## THE FAITH OF THE ACCEPTABLE OFFERING

*Hebrews* 11 : 4

It was by faith that Abel offered to God a fuller sacrifice than Cain
and so gained the verdict of being a just man, for God himself
witnessed to that fact on the grounds of the gifts he brought: and
although he died because of his faith, he is still speaking to us.

THE writer to the Hebrews begins his honour roll of faith with
the name of Abel whose story is in *Genesis* 4: 1–15. Cain tilled
the ground and brought to God an offering of the fruits of the
ground; Abel was a flock-master and brought to God an
offering from his flocks. God preferred the gift of Abel to the
gift of Cain who, moved to bitter jealousy, murdered his
brother and became an outcast upon the earth. In the original,
the meaning of the story is difficult. There is no indication why
God preferred the gift of Abel to the gift of Cain. It may well
be that the only offering which a man can properly bring to
God is his most precious possession. This is *life itself*; and to
the Hebrews blood always stood for life. We can well understand that, because when the blood flows away, life ebbs away.
On that principle the only true sacrifice to God was a sacrifice
of blood. Abel's sacrifice was of a living creature, Cain's was
not; therefore Abel's was the more acceptable.

But it may well be that the writer to the Hebrews is thinking
not only of the story as it is in Genesis but also of the legends
which gathered round it in Jewish folk-lore. The Jews themselves found the story puzzling and elaborated it in order to
find a reason for God's rejection of Cain and for Cain's murder
of Abel. The earliest legend tells how every time Eve bore
children she bore twins, a boy and a girl, and that they were
given to each other as man and wife. In the case of Abel and

Cain, Adam tried to change this and planned to give the twin sister of Cain to Abel. Cain was bitterly dissatisfied. To settle the matter, Adam said to them: "Go, my sons, sacrifice to the Lord; and he whose sacrifice is accepted shall have the young girl. Take each of you offerings in your hand and go, sacrifice to the Lord and he will decide." So Abel, who was a shepherd, took his best lamb to the place of sacrifice; but Cain, who was a tiller of the ground, took the poorest sheaf of corn he could find and laid it on the altar. Whereupon fire descended from heaven and consumed Abel's offering so that not even the cinders were left while Cain's was left untouched. Adam then gave the girl to Abel and Cain was sorely vexed. One day Abel was asleep upon a mountain; and Cain came upon him and took a stone and crushed his head. Then he threw the dead body on his back and carried it about because he did not know what to do with it. He saw two crows fighting and one killed the other, then dug a hole with its beak and buried it. Cain said: "I have not the sense of this bird. I, too, will lay my brother in the ground," and he did so.

The Jews had still another story to explain the first murder. Cain and Abel could not agree as to what they should possess. So Abel devised a scheme whereby they might bring an end to contention. Cain took the earth and everything stationary; Abel took everything moveable. But in Cain's heart there was still bitter envy. One day he said to his brother: "Remove thy foot; thou standest on my property; the plain is mine." Abel ran to the hills but Cain pursued him, saying: "The hills are mine." Abel took refuge on the mountains but Cain still pursued him saying: "The mountains, too, are mine." And so, in his envy, he hunted his brother until he killed him.

At the back of this story lie two great truths. First, there is *envy*. Even the Greeks saw its horror. Demosthenes said: "Envy is the sign of a nature that is altogether evil." Euripides said: "Envy is the greatest of all diseases among men." There was a Greek proverb which said: "Envy has no place in the choir of God." Envy leads to bitterness; bitterness to hatred; and hatred to murder. Envy is that poison which can poison all life and kill all goodness. Second, there is this strange and eerie thought that Cain had discovered a new sin. One of the old Greek fathers said: "Up to this time no man had died so that Cain should know how to kill. The devil instructed him in this in a dream." It was Cain who introduced murder into the world. There is condemnation for the sinner; but there is still greater condemnation for the man who teaches another to sin. Such a man, even as Cain was, is banished from the face of God.

So the writer to the Hebrews says: "Although he died for his faith, he is still speaking to us." Moffatt finely comments: "Death is never the last word in the life of a righteous man." When a man leaves this world, he leaves something in it. He may leave something which will grow and spread like a canker; or he may leave something fine which blossoms and flourishes without end. He leaves an influence of good or ill; every one when he dies still speaks. May God grant to us to leave behind not a germ of evil but a lovely thing in which the lives of those who come afterwards will find blessing.

## WALKING WITH GOD

*Hebrews* 11: 5, 6

It was by faith that Enoch was transferred from this to the other life so that he did not die but passed from men's sight, because God took him from one life to the other. For, before this change came to him it was testified that he pleased God. Apart from faith it is impossible to please God, for he who approaches God must believe that God is, and that he is the rewarder of those who spend their lives seeking him.

IN the Old Testament the life of Enoch is summed up in one sentence: "And Enoch walked with God; and he was not, for God took him" (*Genesis* 5: 24). Many legends gathered around his name. He was said to be the first man skilled in tailoring and in sewing and that he instructed men how to cut out skins in the proper shape to make garments.

He was said to be the first to teach men to make shoes to protect their feet. He was said to be the first to put pen to paper and instruct men from books.

Legend tells that with Enoch the Angel of Death made a compact of friendship. Enoch made three requests of him. First, to die and come back again so that he might know what death was like. Second, to see the abode of the wicked so that he might know what the punishment of the evil was like. Both these requests were granted. His third request was to be permitted to see into Paradise so that he might see what the blessed enjoyed. This also was granted, but Enoch, having been granted a glimpse of Paradise, never came back to earth again.

The simple statement in Genesis has a kind of mystical quality. In itself it does not say how Enoch died. It simply says that in God's good time he passed serenely from this earth. There were two specially famous interpretations of the death of Enoch.

(i) *The Book of Wisdom* (4: 10ff.) has the idea that God took Enoch to himself when he was still young to save him from the infection of this world. "He was taken away while he lived amidst sinners. . . . He was snatched away lest evil should change his understanding or guile deceive his soul." This is another way of putting the famous classical saying: "Whom the gods love die young." It looks on death as a reward. It means that God loved Enoch so much that he removed him before age and degeneration descended hand in hand upon him.

(ii) Philo, the great Alexandrian Jewish interpreter, saw in Enoch the great pattern of *repentance*. He was changed by repentance from the life that is apart from God to the life that walks with God.

The writer to the Hebrews reads into the simple statement of the Old Testament passage the idea that Enoch did not die at all but that in some mystic way God took him to himself. But surely the meaning is much simpler. In a wicked and corrupt generation Enoch walked with God and so when the end came to him, there was no shock or interruption. Death merely took him into God's nearer presence. Because he walked with God when other men were walking away from him, he daily came nearer to him and death was no more than the last step that took him into the very presence of that God with whom he had always walked.

We cannot think of Enoch without thinking of the different attitudes to death. The sheer serenity of the Old Testament statement, so simple and yet so moving, points forward to the Christian attitude.

(i) There are those who have thought of death as *mysterious and inexplicable*. William Morris wrote:

"Death have we hated, knowing not what it meant."

Bacon said: "Men fear death as children fear to go in the dark." To some, it has always been the terrifying unknown giving rise to what Hamlet called "that dread of something after death."

(ii) There are those who simply have seen in death *the one inevitable thing in life*. Shakespeare makes Caesar say in *Julius Caesar*:

"It seems to me most strange that men should fear;
    Seeing that death, a necessary end,
    Will come when it will come."

And in *Cymbeline* he writes with a strange fatalistic beauty:

"Fear no more the heat o' the sun,
    Nor the furious winter's rages;
Thou thy worldly task hast done,
    Home art gone and ta'en thy wages:
Golden lads and girls all must,
As chimney-sweepers, come to dust.

"Fear no more the frown o' the great,
    Thou art past the tyrant's stroke:
Care no more to clothe and eat;
    To thee the reed is as the oak:
The sceptre, learning, physic must
All follow this, and come to dust.

> "Fear not more the lightning-flash,
>    Nor the all-dreaded thunder-stone;
> Fear not slander, censure rash;
>    Thou hast finish'd joy and moan:
> All lovers young, all lovers must
> Consign to thee, and come to dust."

Death is inevitable and there is nothing to be gained by struggling against it.

(iii) Some have seen in death *sheer extinction.* It was that loveliest of Roman poets, Catullus, who pled with Lesbia for her kisses because the night was coming:

> "Lesbia mine, let's live and love!
> Give no doit for tattle of
> Crabbed old censorious men;
> Suns may set and rise again,
> But when our short day takes flight
> Sleep we must one endless night."

To die was to go out to nothingness and be lost in an eternal sleep.

(iv) Some have seen in death *the supreme terror and the unmitigated evil.* In *Measure for Measure* Shakespeare makes Claudio say:

> "Death is a fearful thing.
> Ay, but to die, and go we know not where;
> To lie in cold obstruction, and to rot;
> This sensible warm motion to become
> A kneaded clod; and the delighted spirit
> To bathe in fiery floods, or to reside
> In thrilling region of thick-ribbed ice;
> To be imprison'd in the viewless winds,
> And blown with restless violence round about
> The pendent world. . . .
> The weariest and most loathed worldly life
> That age, ache, penury and imprisonment
> Can lay on nature, is a paradise
> To what we fear of death."

To Claudio the worst and bitterest of life was to be preferred to death. W. S. Gilbert wrote in *The Yeomen of the Guard:*

> "Is life a boon?
> If so, it must befall
> That Death, whene'er he call,
> Must call too soon."

Robert Burns wrote of the early death of Highland Mary:

> "But oh! fell death's untimely frost
> That nipt my flower sae early!"

There are those who have seen only the grim terroriser and despoiler in death.

(v) Many have seen in death *release*. Weary of the world and of life, they have seen it as escape. Keats said that he had been "half in love with easeful death." Shakespeare in one of his sonnets cried:

> "Tir'd with all these, for restful death I cry."

Nicholas Rowe wrote: "Death is the privilege of human nature." The Stoics held that the gods had given men the gift of life and the still greater gift of taking their own lives away. Swinburne best of all caught this mood of world-weariness in *The Garden of Proserpine*:

> "From too much love of living,
>     From hope and fear set free,
> We thank with brief thanksgiving
>     Whatever gods may be
> That no life lives forever,
> That dead men rise up never;
> That even the weariest river
>     Winds somewhere safe to sea.
>
> Then star nor sun shall waken,
>     Nor any change of light;
> Nor sound of waters shaken,
>     Nor any sound or sight;
> Nor wintry leaves nor vernal
> Nor days nor things diurnal;
> Only the sleep eternal
>     In an eternal night."

There are those for whom death is good because it is the end of life.

(vi) Some have seen in death *transition*—not an end, but a stage on the way; not a door closing, but a door opening. Longfellow wrote:

> "There is no Death! What seems so is transition;
> This life of mortal breath
> Is but a suburb of the life elysian,
> Whose portal we call death."

George Meredith wrote:

> "Death met I too,
> And saw the dawn glow through."

To such death has always been a call to come up higher, a crossing from the dark to the dawn.

(vii) Some have seen death as an *adventure*. As Barrie made Peter Pan say: "To die will be an awfully big adventure." Charles Frohman, who had known Barrie so well, went down with the *Lusitania* in that disaster of 7 May 1915. His last words were: "Why fear death? It is the most beautiful adventure in life." An old scholar who was dying turned to his friends: "Do you realize," he said, "that in an hour or two I will know the answers for which we have been searching all our lives?" To such death is the adventure of supreme discovery.

(viii) Above all, there are those, like Enoch, who have seen death as an *entering into the nearer presence* of him with whom they have lived for so long. If we have lived with Christ, we may die in the certainty that we go to be for ever with our Lord.

In this passage the writer to the Hebrews lays down in addition the two great foundation acts of faith of the Christian life.

(i) *We must believe in God.* There can be no such thing as religion without that belief. Religion began when men became aware of God; it ceases when they live a life in which for them God does not exist.

(ii) *We must believe that God is interested.* As the writer to the Hebrews put it, we must believe that God is the rewarder of those who diligently seek him.

There were those in the ancient world who believed in the gods, but they believed that they lived out in the spaces between the worlds, entirely unaware of these strange animals called men. "God," said Epicurus as a first principle, "does nothing." There are many who believe in God but do not believe that he cares. It has been said that no astronomer can be an atheist; but it has also been said that an astronomer is bound to believe that God is a mathematician. But a God who is a mathematician need not care. Men have called God The First Principle, The First Cause, The Creative Energy, The Life Force. These are the statements of men who believe in God, but not in a God who cares.

When Marcus Aurelius was asked why he believed in the gods, he said: "True, the gods are not discernible by human sight, but neither have I seen my soul and yet I honour it. So then I believe in the gods and I honour them, because again and again I have experienced their power." Not logic but life convinced him of the gods. Seneca said: "The first essential of the worship of the gods is to believe that there are gods . . . and to know those gods who preside over the world, because they control the universe with their power, and work for the safety of the whole human race, while they still remember each individual person." Epictetus said: "You must know that the most important thing in reverence for the gods is to have right beliefs that they are and that they order all things righteously and well."

We must believe not only that God exists but also that he cares and is involved in the human situation. For the Christian that is easy, for God came to the world in Jesus Christ to tell us how much he cares.

## THE MAN WHO BELIEVED IN GOD'S MESSAGE

*Hebrews* 11:7

It was by faith that Noah, when he had been informed by God about things that were still unseen, reverently accepted the message and built an ark to preserve his household in safety. Through that

faith he passed judgment on the world and became an heir of the
righteousness which is the result of faith.

THE Old Testament story of Noah is in *Genesis* chapters 6 to 8.
The earth was so wicked that God decided that there remained
nothing to do but destroy it. He told Noah his purpose of
judgment and instructed him to build an ark in which he
and his family and the representatives of the animal creation
might be saved. With reverence and obedience Noah took
God at his word and so in the destruction of the world he was
preserved.

As is usually the case, legend adds many a detail to this
story. The writer to the Hebrews must have known these
legends and they must have helped to add vividness to the
picture in his mind. One story tells how Noah was in doubt
as to the shape he was to give the ark. God revealed to him
that it was to be modelled on a bird's belly and was to be
constructed of teak wood. Noah planted a teak tree and in
twenty years it grew to such a size that out of it he was able to
build the entire ark. Another story tells that, after he had been
forewarned by God, Noah made a bell of plane wood, about
five feet high, and that he sounded it every day, morning,
noon and evening. When he was asked why, he answered:
"To warn you that God will send a deluge to destroy you
all." Another story tells that, when Noah was building the
ark, the people laughed at him and counted him mad. But
he said to them: "Though you rail at me now, the time will
come when I shall rail at you; for you will learn to your cost
who it is that punishes the wicked in this world and reserves
for them a further punishment in the world to come."

Even more than Abel and Enoch, Noah stands out as a
man of faith.

(i) *Noah took God at his word.* He believed the message
which God sent him. God's message might look foolishness
at the moment; but Noah believed it and staked everything
on it. Obviously if he was going to accept that word of God,
he had to lay aside his normal activities and concentrate on
doing what his message commanded. Noah's life was one

continued and concentrated preparation for what God had said would come.

The choice comes to every man either to listen to or to disregard the message of God. He may live as if that message is of no importance or as if it is the most important thing in the world. We may put it in another way—Noah was the man who heeded the warning of God; and because he heeded he was saved from disaster. God's warning comes to us in many ways. It may come from conscience; it may come from some direct word of God to our souls; it may come from the advice or the rebuke of some good and godly man; it may leap out at us from God's Book or challenge us in some sermon. Wherever it comes from, we neglect it at our peril.

(ii) *Noah was not deterred by the mockery of others.* When the sun was shining, his conduct must have looked like that of a fool. Who ever in his senses built a great hulk of a ship on dry land far from the sea? The man who takes God's word may often have to adopt a course of action which looks like madness.

We have only to think of the early days of the Church. One man meets a friend. He says to him: "I have decided to become a Christian." The other man replies: "Do you know what happens to Christians? They are outlaws. They are imprisoned, thrown to the lions, crucified, burned." The first man replies: "I know." And the other says despairingly: " You must be mad."

It is one of the hardest challenges of Christianity that we have to be prepared to be sometimes a fool for Jesus's sake. We should never forget that there was a day when his friends came and tried to get him to go home because they thought that he was mad. The wisdom of God is so often foolishness with men.

(iii) *Noah's faith was a judgment on others.* That is why, at least in one sense, it is dangerous to be a Christian. It is not that the Christian is self-righteous; it is not that he is censorious; it is not that he goes about finding fault with other people; it is not that he says: "I told you so." It often

happens that simply by being himself the Christian passes
judgment on other people. Alcibiades that brilliant but
wild young man of Athens used to say to Socrates:
"Socrates, I hate you, for every time I meet you, you show
me what I am." One of the finest men who ever lived in
Athens was Aristides, who was called "the just." But they
voted to banish him. One man, asked why he had so voted,
answered: "Because I am tired of hearing Aristides called
'the just.'" There is danger in goodness, for in its light evil
stands condemned.

(iv) *Noah was righteous through faith.* It so happens that
he is the first man in the Bible to be called *dikaios, righteous*
(*Genesis* 6: 9). His goodness consisted in the fact that he took
God at his word. When other men broke God's commandments, Noah kept them; when other men were deaf to God's
warnings, Noah listened to them; when other men laughed at
God, Noah reverenced him. It has been said of Noah that
"he threw the dark scepticism of the world into relief
against his own shining faith in God." In an age when men
disregarded God, for Noah he was the supreme reality in the
world.

## THE ADVENTURE AND THE PATIENCE OF FAITH

*Hebrews* 11: 8–10

> It was by faith that Abraham, when he was called, showed his
> obedience by going out to a place which he was going to receive
> as an inheritance, and he went out not knowing where he was to go.
> It was by faith that he sojourned in the land that had been
> promised to him, as though it had been a foreign land, living
> in tents, in the same way as did Isaac and Jacob, who were his
> coheirs in the promise of it. For he was waiting for the city which
> has foundations, whose architect and builder is God.

THE call of Abraham is told with dramatic simplicity in
*Genesis* 12: 1. Jewish and eastern legends gathered largely
round Abraham's name and some of them must have been

known to the writer to the Hebrews. The legends tell how
Abraham was the son of Terah, commander of the armies
of Nimrod. When Abraham was born a very vivid star appeared
in the sky and seemed to obliterate the others. Nimrod
sought to murder the infant but Abraham was concealed
in a cave and his life saved. It was in that cave the first vision
of God came to him. When he was a youth he came out
of the cave and stood looking across the face of the desert.
The sun rose in all its glory and Abraham said: "Surely the
sun is God, the Creator!" So he knelt down and worshipped
the sun. But when evening came, the sun sank in the west and
Abraham said: "No! the author of creation cannot set!"
The moon arose in the east and the stars came out. Then
Abraham said: "The moon must be God and the stars his
host!" So he knelt down and adored the moon. But after
the night was passed, the moon sank and the sun rose again
and Abraham said: "Truly these heavenly bodies are no
gods, for they obey law; I will worship him who imposed the
law upon them."

The Arabs have a different legend. They tell how Abraham
saw many flocks and herds and said to his mother: "Who
is the lord of these?" She answered: "Your father, Terah."
"And who is the lord of Terah?" the lad Abraham asked.
"Nimrod," said his mother. "And who is the lord of Nimrod?"
asked Abraham. His mother bade him be quite and not
push questions too far; but already Abraham's thoughts were
reaching out to him who is the God of all. The legends go on
to tell that Terah not only worshipped twelve idols, one for
each of the months, but was also a manufacturer of idols.
One day Abraham was left in charge of the shop. People came
in to buy idols. Abraham would ask them how old they were
and they would answer perhaps fifty or sixty years of age.
"Woe to a man of such an age," said Abraham, "who adores
the work of one day!" A strong and hale man of seventy came
in. Abraham asked him his age and then said: "You fool
to adore a god who is younger than yourself!" A woman came
in with a dish of meat for the gods. Abraham took a stick and

smashed all the idols but one, in whose hands he set the stick he had used. Terah returned and was angry. Abraham said: "My father, a woman brought this dish of meat for your gods; they all wanted to have it and the strongest knocked the heads off the rest, lest they should eat it all." Terah said: "That is impossible for they are made of wood and stone." And Abraham answered: "Let thine own ear hear what thine own mouth has spoken!"

All these legends give us a vivid picture of Abraham searching after God and dissatisfied with the idolatry of his people. So when God's call came to him he was ready to go out into the unknown to find him! Abraham is the supreme example of faith.

(i) Abraham's faith was *the faith that was ready for adventure*. God's summons meant that he had to leave home and family and business; yet he went. He had to go out into the unknown; yet he went. In the best of us there is a certain timorousness. We wonder just what will happen to us if we take God at his word and act on his commands and promises.

Bishop Newbigin tells of the negotiations which led to the formation of the United Church of South India. He had a share in these negotiations and in the long discussions which were necessary. Things were frequently held up by cautious people who wished to know just where each step was taking them, until in the end the chairman reminded them that a Christian has no right to ask where he is going.

Most of us live a cautious life on the principle of safety first; but to live the Christian life there is necessary a certain reckless willingness to adventure. If faith can see every step of the way, it is not really faith. It is sometimes necessary for the Christian to take the way to which the voice of God is calling him without knowing what the consequences will be. Like Abraham he has to go out not knowing where he is going.

(ii) Abraham's faith was *the faith which had patience*. When he reached the promised land, he was never allowed to possess it. He had to wander in it, a stranger and a tent-dweller, as the people were some day to wander in the wilderness. To Abraham God's promise never came fully true; and yet he never abandoned his faith.

It is characteristic of the best of us that we are in a hurry. To wait is even harder than to adventure. The hardest time of all is the time in between. At the moment of decision there is the excitement and the thrill; at the moment of achievement there is the glow and glory of satisfaction; but in the intervening time there is necessary the ability to wait and work and watch when nothing seems to be happening. It is then that we are so liable to give up our hopes and lower our ideals and sink into an apathy whose dreams are dead. The man of faith is the man whose hope is flaming bright and whose effort is intensely strenuous even in the grey days when there is nothing to do but to wait.

(iii) Abraham's faith was *the faith which was looking beyond this world*. The later legends believed that at the moment of his call Abraham was given a glimpse of the new Jerusalem. In the *Apocalypse of Baruch* God says: "I showed it to my servant by night" (4: 4). In 4 *Ezra* the writer says: "It came to pass when they practised ungodliness before thee, that thou didst choose one from among them whose name was Abraham; him thou didst love and to him only thou didst reveal the end of the times, secretly, by night" (4: 13). No man ever did anything great without a vision which enabled him to face the difficulties and discouragements of the way. To Abraham there was given the vision; and, even when his body was wandering in Palestine, his soul was at home with God. God cannot give us the vision unless we permit him; but if we wait upon him, even in earth's desert places he will send us the vision and with it the toil and trouble of the way become all worth while.

## BELIEVING THE INCREDIBLE

*Hebrews* 11 : 11, 12

It was by faith that Sarah, too, received power to conceive and to bear a son, although she was beyond the age for it, for she believed that he who gave the promise could be absolutely relied upon. So from one man, and he a man whose body had lost its vitality, there were born descendants, as many as the stars of the sky in multitude, as countless as the sand upon the seashore.

THE story of the promise of a son to Abraham and Sarah is told in *Genesis* 17: 15–22; 18: 9–15; 21: 1–8. Its wonder is that both Abraham and Sarah were ninety years old, long past the age of begetting or bearing a child; and yet, according to the old story, that promise was made and came true.

The reaction of Abraham and Sarah to the promise of God followed a threefold course.

(i) It began with sheer *incredulousness*. When Abraham heard the promise he fell upon his face and laughed (*Genesis* 17: 17). When Sarah heard it she laughed within herself (*Genesis* 18: 12). On first hearing of the promises of God, the human reaction often is that this is far too good to be true.

> "How thou canst think so well of us,
>   And be the God thou art,
> Is darkness to my intellect,
>   But sunshine to my heart."

There is no mystery in all creation like the love of God. That he should love men and suffer and die for them is something that staggers us into sheer incredulity. That is why the Christian message is the *gospel, good news*; it is news so good that it is almost impossible to believe it true.

(ii) It passed into *dawning realization*. After the incredulity came the dawning realization that *this was God who was speaking*; and God cannot lie. The Jews used to lay it down as a primary law for a teacher that he must never promise his pupils what he was unwilling or unable to

perform; to do so would be to accustom the pupils thus
early to the broken word. When we remember that the one
who makes the promise is *God*, there comes the realization
that however astonishing that promise may be, it must
none the less be true.

(iii) It culminated in *the ability to believe in the impossible.*
That Abraham and Sarah should have a child, humanly
speaking, was impossible. As Sarah said: "Who would have
said that Sarah would suckle children?" (*Genesis* 21: 7). But,
by the grace and the power of God, the impossible became
true. There is something here to challenge and uplift the
heart of every man. Cavour said that the first essential of a
statesman is "the sense of the possible." When we listen
to men planning and arguing and thinking aloud, we get the
impression of a vast number of things in this world which
are known to be desirable but dismissed as impossible. Men
spend the greater part of their lives putting limitations on the
power of God. Faith is the ability to lay hold on that grace
which is sufficient for all things in such a way that the things
which are humanly impossible become divinely possible.
With God all things are possible, and, therefore, the word
impossible has no place in the vocabulary of the Christian
and of the Christian Church.

## SOJOURNERS AND STRANGERS

*Hebrews* 11: 13–16

All these died without obtaining possession of the promises.
They only saw them from far away and greeted them from afar,
and they admitted that they were strangers and sojourners upon
the earth. Now people who speak like that make it quite clear
that they are searching for a fatherland. If they were thinking
of the land from which they had come out, they would have had
time to return. In point of fact they were reaching out after something
better, I mean, the heavenly country. It was because of that
that God was not ashamed to be called their God, for he had
prepared a city for them.

NONE of the patriarchs entered into the full possession of the promises that God had made to Abraham. To the end of their days they were nomads, never living a settled life in a settled land. They had to be for ever moving on. Certain great permanent truths emerge from them.

(i) They lived for ever as strangers. The writer to the Hebrews uses three vivid Greek words about them.

(a) In 11: 13 he calls them *xenoi*. *Xenos* is the word for *a stranger and a foreigner*. In the ancient world the fate of the stranger was hard. He was regarded with hatred and suspicion and contempt. In Sparta *xenos* was the equivalent of *barbaros,* barbarian. A man writes complaining that he was despised "because I am a *xenos*". Another man writes that, however poor a home is, it is better to live at home than *epi xenēs,* in a foreign country. When clubs had their common meal, those who sat down to it were divided into *members* and *xenoi*. *Xenos* can even mean a *refugee*. All their lives the patriarchs were foreigners in a land that never was their own.

(b) In 11: 9 he uses the word *paroikein, to sojourn,* of Abraham. A *paroikos* was *a resident alien*. The word is used of the Jews when they were captives in Babylon and in Egypt. A *paroikos* was not very much above a slave in the social scale. He had to pay an alien tax. He was always an outsider and only on payment a member of the community.

(c) In 11: 13 he uses the word *parepidēmos*. A *parepidēmos* was a person who was staying there temporarily and who had his permanent home somewhere else. Sometimes his stay was strictly limited. A *parepidēmos* was a man in lodgings, a man without a home in the place where life had sent him. All their lives the patriarchs were men who had no settled place that they could call home. It is to be noted that to dwell in a foreign land was a humiliating thing in ancient days; to the foreigner in any country a certain stigma attached. In the *Letter of Aristeas* the writer says: "It is a fine thing to live and to die in one's native land; a foreign land brings contempt to poor men and shame to rich men, for there is the lurking suspicion that they have been exiled for the

evil they have done." In *Ecclesiasticus* (29: 22–28) there is a
wistful passage:

> "Better the life of the poor under a shelter of logs
>    Than sumptuous fare in the house of strangers.
> With little or much be contented:
>    So wilt thou not have to bear the reproach of thy wandering.
>
> An evil life it is to go from house to house,
>    And where thou art a stranger thou must not open thy mouth.
> A stranger thou art in that case and drinkest contempt;
>    And besides this thou wilt have to hear bitter things:
> 'Come hither, sojourner, and furnish my table,
>    And if thou hast aught feed me therewith';
> Or, 'Get thee gone, sojourner, from the face of honour,
>    My brother is come as my guest, I have need of my house.'
> These things are grievous to a man of understanding:
>    Upbraiding concerning sojourning, and the reproach of a
>    moneylender."

At any time it is an unhappy thing to be a stranger in a
strange land, but in ancient days to this natural unhappiness
there was added the bitterness of humiliation.

All their days the patriarchs were strangers in a strange land.
That picture of the sojourner became a picture of the Christian
life. Tertullian said of the Christian: "He knows that on earth
he has a pilgrimage but that his dignity is in heaven." Clement
of Alexandria said: "We have no fatherland on earth."
Augustine said: "We are sojourners exiled from our fatherland." It was not that the Christians were foolishly other-
worldly, detaching themselves from the life and work of this
world; but they always remembered that they were people on
the way. There is an unwritten saying of Jesus: "The world
is a bridge. The wise man will pass over it but will not build
his house upon it." The Christian regards himself as the pilgrim
of eternity.

(ii) In spite of everything these men never lost their vision
and their hope. However long that hope might be in coming
true, its light always shone in their eyes. However long the
way might be, they never stopped tramping along it. Robert

Louis Stevenson said: "It is better to travel hopefully than to arrive." They never wearily gave up the journey; they lived in hope and died in expectation.

(iii) In spite of everything they never wished to go back. Their descendants, when they were in the desert, often wished to go back to the fleshpots of Egypt. But not the patriarchs. They had begun and it never struck them to turn back. In flying there is what is called *the point of no return*. When the aeroplane has reached that point *it cannot go back*. Its petrol supply has reached such a level that there is nothing left but to go on. One of the tragedies of life is the number of people who turn back just a little too soon. One further effort, a little more waiting, a little more hoping, would make the dream come true. Immediately a Christian has set out on some enterprise sent him by God, he should feel that he has already passed the point of no return.

(iv) These men were able to go on because they were haunted by the things beyond. The man with the wanderlust is lured on by the thought of the countries he has never yet seen. The great artist or composer is driven by the thought of the performance he has never yet given and the wonder he has never yet produced. Stevenson tells of an old byreman who spent all his days amidst the muck of the byre. Someone asked him if he never got tired of it all. He answered: "He that has something ayont (beyond) need never weary." These men had the something beyond—and so may we.

(v) Because these men were what they were, God was not ashamed to be called their God. Above all things, he is the God of the gallant adventurer. He loves the man who is ready to venture for his name. The prudent, comfort-loving man is the very opposite of God. The man who goes out into the unknown and keeps going on will in the end arrive at God.

### THE SUPREME SACRIFICE

*Hebrews* 11: 17–19

It was by faith that Abraham offered up Isaac when he was put to

the test. He was willing to offer up even his only son, although it
had been said to him: "It is in Isaac that your descendants will be
named." He was willing to do this for he reckoned that God was
able to raise him even from the dead. Hence he did receive him
back which is a parable of the resurrection.

THE Isaac story, told in *Genesis* 22: 1–18, is that most dramatic
account of how Abraham met the supreme test of the demand
for the life of his own son. To some extent this story has fallen
into disrepute. It is excluded from syllabuses of religious
education because it is held to teach an unacceptable view of
God. Or it is held that the point of the story is that it was in
this way that Abraham learned that God did not desire human
sacrifice. No doubt that is true; but, if we want to see this story
at its greatest and as the writer to the Hebrews saw it, we must
take it at its face value. It was the response of a man who was
asked to offer God his own son.

(i) This story teaches us that we must be ready to sacrifice
what is dearest to us for the sake of loyalty to God. There
have been many who have sacrificed their careers to what they
took to be the will of God. J. P. Struthers was the minister of
the Reformed Presbyterian Church in Greenock, a little congregation, which, it is neither false nor unkind to say, had a
great past but no future. Had he been willing to forsake the
Church of his fathers, any pulpit in the land was open to him
and the most dazzling ecclesiastical prizes were his; but he
sacrificed them all for the sake of what he considered to be
loyalty to God's will.

Sometimes a man may have to sacrifice personal relationships. He may feel called by God to a task in a sphere which
is difficult and in a place that is unattractive and it may be that
the girl he is to marry will not face it with him. The man
must choose between the will of God and the relationship
which means so much to him. When Bunyan was in gaol he
was thinking of what must happen to his family if he was
executed. Especially the thought of his little blind daughter,
who was so dear to him, haunted him: "O," he said, "I saw
in this condition I was a man who was pulling down his house

upon the head of his wife and children; yet, thought I, I must
do it, I must do it."

> "The dearest idol I have known,
>   Whate'er that idol be,
> Help me to tear it from thy throne,
>   And worship only thee."

Abraham was the man who would sacrifice even the dearest
thing in life for God. Time and again in the early Church
it happened. In a home one partner became a Christian and
the other did not; the children became Christians and the
parents did not. The sword came down upon that home; and
unless there had been those who counted Christ dearer than
all else, there would be no Christianity today.

God must come first in our lives, or he comes nowhere.
There is a story of two children who had been given a toy
Noah's Ark as a present. They had been listening to the Old
Testament stories and determined that they too would offer a
sacrifice. They examined the animals in their toy ark and finally
decided on *a sheep with a broken leg.* The only thing they would
offer was a broken toy they could well do without. That is the
way in which so many people would like to sacrifice to God;
but only the dearest and the best is good enough for him.

(ii) Abraham is the pattern of the man who accepts what
he cannot understand. To him there had come this incom-
prehensible demand. It did not make sense. The promise was
that in Isaac his seed would grow and grow until he became a
mighty nation in which all others would be blessed. On the life
of Isaac depended the promise; and now God seemed to want
to take that life away. As Chrysostom put it: "The things of
God seemed to fight against the things of God, and faith fought
with faith, and the commandment fought with the promise."
For everyone at some time there comes something for which
there seems to be no reason and which defies explanation. It is
then that a man is faced with life's hardest battle—to accept
when he cannot understand. At such a time there is only one
thing to do—to obey and to do so without resentment, saying:
"God, you are love! I build my faith on that."

(iii) Abraham is the pattern of the man who. with the test, found a way of escape. If we take God at his word and stake everything on him. even when there seems to be nothing but a blank wall in front of us. the way of escape will open up.

## THE FAITH WHICH DEFEATS DEATH

*Hebrews* 11: 20–22

> It was by faith that Isaac blessed Jacob and Esau in the things concerning the future. It was by faith that Jacob, when he was dying, blessed each of the sons of Joseph and prayed leaning on the head of his staff. It was by faith that Joseph. as he came to the end. had in his mind the days when the children of Israel would leave Egypt, and gave instructions concerning his bones.

ONE thing links these three examples of faith together. In each case it was the faith of a man to whom death was very near. The blessing which Isaac gave is in *Genesis* 27: 28, 29, 39, 40. Given after Isaac had said: "Behold, I am old, I do not know the day of my death" (*Genesis* 27: 2), it was: "God give you of the dew of heaven, and of the fatness of the earth and plenty of grain and wine. Let peoples serve you and nations bow down to you." The blessing of Jacob is given in *Genesis* 48: 9–22. The story has just said that "the time drew near that Israel must die" (*Genesis* 47: 29). The blessing was: "In them let my name be perpetuated, and the name of my fathers Abraham and Isaac; and let them grow into a multitude in the midst of the earth" (*Genesis* 48: 15, 16). The incident from the life of Joseph comes from *Genesis* 50: 22–26. When Joseph was near to death he made the Israelites take an oath that they would not leave his bones in Egypt but would take them with them when they went out to possess the promised land, which in due time they did (*Exodus* 13: 19; *Joshua* 24: 32).

The point which the writer to the Hebrews wishes to make is that all three men died without having entered into the promise that God had made, the promise of the Promised Land

and of greatness to the nation of Israel. Isaac was still a nomad, Jacob was an exile in Egypt, Joseph had attained to greatness but it was the greatness of a stranger in a strange land; and yet they never doubted that the promise would come true. They died not in despair but in hope. Their faith defeated death.

There is something of permanent greatness here. The thought in the mind of all these men was the same: "God's promise is true, for he never breaks a promise. I may not live to see it, death may come to me before that promise becomes a fact; but I am a link in its fulfilment. Whether or not that promise comes depends on me." Here is the great function of life. Our hopes may never be realized but we must live in such a way that we shall hasten their coming. It may not be given to every man to enter into the fullness of the promises of God, but it is given to him to live with such fidelity as to bring nearer the day when others will enter into it. To us all is given the tremendous task of helping God make his promises come true.

## FAITH AND ITS SECRET

*Hebrews* 11: 23–29

It was by faith that Moses, when he was born, was kept hidden for three months by his parents, because they saw that the child was beautiful: and they did not fear the edict of the king. It was by faith that Moses, when he grew to manhood, refused to be called the son of Pharaoh's daughter and chose rather to suffer evil with the people of God than to enjoy the transient pleasures of sin, for he considered that a life of reproach for the sake of the Messiah was greater wealth than the treasures of Egypt, for he kept his eyes fixed upon his reward. It was by faith that he left Egypt, unmoved by the blazing anger of the king, for he could face all things as one who sees him who is invisible. It was by faith that he carried out the Passover and the sprinkling of blood, so that the destroying angel might not touch the children of his people. It was by faith that they crossed the Red Sea as if they were going through dry land and that the Egyptians, when they ventured to try to do so, were engulfed.

To the Hebrews Moses was the supreme figure in their history. He was the leader who had rescued them from slavery and who had received the Law of their lives from God. To the writer of the letter to the Hebrews Moses was pre-eminently the man of faith. In this story, as Moffatt points out, there are five different acts of faith. As with the other great characters whose names are included in this roll of honour of God's faithful ones, many legends and elaborations had gathered round the name of Moses and doubtless the writer of this letter had them also in his mind.

(i) There was the faith of Moses's parents. The story of their action is told in *Exodus* 2: 1–10. *Exodus* 1: 15–22 tells how the king of Egypt in his hatred tried to wipe out the children of the Israelites by having them killed at birth. Legend tells how Amram and Jochebed, the parents of Moses (*Exodus* 6: 20), were troubled by the decree of Pharaoh. As a result Amram put away his wife, not because he did not love her, but because he would spare her the sorrow of seeing her children killed. For three years she was put away, and then Miriam prophesied: "My parents shall have another son, who shall deliver Israel out of the hands of the Egyptians." She said to her father: "What hast thou done? Thou hast sent thy wife away out of thine house, because thou couldst not trust the Lord God that he would protect the child that might be born to thee." So Amram, shamed into trusting God, took back his wife; and in due time Moses was born. He was so lovely a child that his parents determined to hide him in their house. This they did for three months. Then, the legend tells, the Egyptians struck upon a cruel scheme. The king was determined that hidden children should be sought out and killed. Now when a child hears another child cry, he will cry too. So Egyptian mothers were sent into the homes of the Israelites with their babies; there they pricked their babies until they cried. This made the hidden children of the Israelites cry, too, and so they were discovered and killed. In view of this, Amram and Jochebed decided to make a little ark and to entrust their child to it on the waters of the Nile.

That Moses was born at all was an act of faith; that he was preserved was another. He began by being the child of faith.

(ii) The second act of faith was Moses's loyalty to his own people. The story is told in *Exodus* 2: 11–14. Again the legends help to light up the picture. When Moses was entrusted to the waters of the Nile, he was found by the daughter of Pharaoh, whose name is given as Bithia, or more commonly Thermouthis. She was entranced by his beauty. Legend says that when she drew the ark out of the water, the archangel Gabriel boxed the ears of the little baby to make him cry so that the heart of Thermouthis might be touched as she saw the little face puckered in sorrow and the eyes full of tears. Thermouthis, much to her sorrow, was childless; so she took the baby Moses home, and cared for him as her own son. He grew to be so beautiful that people turned in the street, and even ceased their work, to look at him. He was so wise that he was far beyond all other children in learning and in knowledge. When he was still a child, Thermouthis took him to Pharaoh and told him how she had found him. She placed him in his arms, and he was so entranced by the child that he embraced him and, at the request of Thermouthis, he promised to make him his heir. By way of jest he took his crown and placed it on the child's head; but the infant snatched the crown from his head and flung it on the ground and trampled on it. Pharaoh's wise men were full of foreboding that this child would some day trample the royal power under foot. They wished to destroy Moses there and then. But a test was proposed; they set before the child a bowl of precious stones and a bowl of live coals. If he put out his hand and touched the jewels, that would prove that he was so wise that he was a danger; if he put out his hands and touched the coals, that would prove that he was so witless that he was no danger. The infant Moses was about to touch the jewels when Gabriel took his hand and put it on the coals. His finger was burnt; he put the burnt finger in his mouth and burnt his mouth; that, they say, was why he was not a good speaker (*Exodus* 4: 10) but stammered all his life.

So Moses was spared. He was brought up in all luxury. He was heir to the kingdom. He became one of the greatest of all Egyptian generals; in particular he conquered the Ethiopians when they were threatening Egypt and in the end was married to an Ethiopian princess. But all the time he had never forgotten his fellow-countrymen; and the day came when he decided to ally himself with the downtrodden Israelites and say goodbye to the future of riches and royalty that he might have had.

Moses gave up earthly glory for the sake of the people of God. Christ gave up his glory for the sake of mankind; and accepted scourging and shame and a terrible death. Moses in his day and generation shared in the sufferings of Christ, choosing the loyalty that led to suffering rather than the ease which led to earthly glory. He knew that the prizes of earth were contemptible compared with the ultimate reward of God.

(iii) There came the day when Moses, because of his intervention on behalf of his people, had to withdraw from Egypt to Midian (*Exodus* 2: 14–22). Because of the order in which it comes that must be what verse 27 refers to. Some people have found difficulty here, because the Exodus narrative says that it was because Moses feared Pharaoh that he fled to Midian (*Exodus* 2: 14), while Hebrews says that he went out not fearing the blazing wrath of the king. There is no real contradiction. It is simply that the writer of the letter to the Hebrews saw even more deeply into the story. For Moses to withdraw to Midian was not an act of fear; it was an act of courage. It showed the courage of the man who has learned to wait.

The Stoics were wise; they held that a man should not throw his life away by needlessly provoking the wrath of a tyrant. Seneca wrote: "The wise man will never provoke the wrath of mighty men; nay, he will turn aside from it; in just the same way as sailors in sailing will not deliberately court the danger of the storm." At that moment Moses might have gone on but his people were not ready. If he had gone on recklessly he would simply have thrown his life away and the deliverance

from Egypt might never have happened. He was big enough
and brave enough to wait until God said: "Now is the hour."

Moffatt quotes a saying of A. S. Peake: "The courage to
abandon work on which one's heart is set and accept inaction
cheerfully as the will of God is of the rarest and highest kind
and can be created and sustained only by the clearest spiritual
vision." When our fighting instincts say: "Go on," it takes a
big and a brave man to wait. It is human to fear to miss the
chance; but it is great to wait for the time of God—even when
it seems like throwing a chance away.

(iv) There came the day when Moses had to make all the
arrangements for the first Passover. The account is in *Exodus*
12: 12–48. The unleavened bread had to be made; the Passover
lamb had to be slain; the door post had to be smeared with
the blood of the lamb so that the Angel of Death would see
the blood and pass over that house and not slay the first-born
in it. But the really amazing thing is that, according to the
Exodus story, Moses not only made these regulations for the
night on which the children of Israel were leaving Israel; he also
laid it down that *they were to be observed annually for all time*.
That is to say, he never doubted the success of the enterprise,
never doubted that the people would be delivered from Egypt
and that some day they would reach the promised land. Here
was a band of wretched Hebrew slaves about to set off on a
journey across an unknown desert to an unknown promised
land and here was the whole power of Egypt hot upon their
heels; yet Moses never doubted that God would bring them
safely through. He was pre-eminently the man who had the
faith that if God gave his people an order he would also give
them the strength to carry it out. Moses knew well that God
does not summon his servants to a great task and leave it at
that; he goes with them every step of the way.

(v) There was the great act of the crossing of the Red Sea.
The story is told in *Exodus* 14. There we read of how the
children of Israel were wondrously enabled to pass through
and of how the Egyptians were engulfed when they tried to do
the same. It was at that moment that the faith of Moses

communicated itself to the people and drove them on when they might well have turned back. Here we have the faith of a leader and of a people who were prepared to attempt the impossible at the command of God, realizing that the greatest barrier in the world is no barrier if God be there to help us overpass it. The book *As in Adam* has this sentence: "The business of life, the way to life, consists in getting over fences, not in lying down and moaning on the hither side." To Moses belonged the faith to attempt what appeared to be the most insurmountable fences in the certainty that God would help the man who refused to turn back and insisted on going on.

Finally, this passage not only tells us of the faith of Moses; it also tells us of *the source of that faith*. Verse 27 tells us that he was able to face all things as one who sees him who is invisible. The outstanding characteristic of Moses was the close intimacy of his relationship with God. In *Exodus* 33: 9–11 we read of how he went into the Tabernacle; "and the Lord used to speak to Moses face to face, as a man speaks to his friend." In *Numbers* 12: 7, 8 we read of God's verdict on him when there were those who were ready to rebel against him: "with him I speak mouth to mouth." To put it simply—the secret of his faith was that Moses knew God personally. To every task he came out from God's presence.

It is told that before a great battle Napoleon would stand in his tent alone; he would send for his commanders to come to him, one by one; when they came in, he would say no word but would look them in the eye and shake them by the hand; and they would go out prepared to die for the general whom they loved. That is like Moses and God. Moses had the faith he had because he knew God in the way he did. When we come to it straight from God's presence, no task can ever defeat us. Our failure and our fear are so often due to the fact that we try to do things alone. The secret of victorious living is to face God before we face men.

## THE FAITH WHICH DEFIED THE FACTS

*Hebrews* 11: 30, 31

It was by faith that the walls of Jericho fell down after they had been encircled for seven days. It was by faith that Rahab, the harlot, did not perish with the disobedient because she had welcomed the scouts in peace.

THE writer to the Hebrews has been citing as examples of faith the great figures of the time before Israel entered into the Promised Land. Now he takes two figures from the period of struggle when the children of Israel were winning a place for themselves within Palestine.

(i) The first is the story of the fall of Jericho. That strange old story is told in *Joshua* 6: 1–20. Jericho was a strong city, barred and fortified. To take it seemed impossible. It was God's commandment that once a day for six days and in silence the people should march round it, led by seven priests marching in front of the ark and bearing trumpets of rams' horn. On the seventh day the priests were to blow upon the trumpets, after the city had been encircled seven times, and the people were to shout with all their might, "and the wall of the city will fall down flat." As the old story tells it, so it happened.

That story left an indelible mark upon the memory of Israel. Centuries after this Judas Maccabaeus and his men were facing the city of Caspis, so secure in its strength that its defenders laughed in their safety. "Wherefore Judas with his company, calling upon the great Lord of the world, who without any rams or engines of war did cast down Jericho in the time of Joshua, gave a fierce assault against the walls and took the city by the will of God" (2 *Maccabees* 12: 13–16). The people never forgot what great things God had done for them and, when some great effort was called for, they nerved themselves for it by remembering them.

Here is the very point the writer to the Hebrews wishes to make. The taking of Jericho was the result of an act of faith. It was taken by men who thought not of what they could do but of what God could do for them. They were prepared to believe that God could make their obvious weakness able for an incredible task. After the smashing of the Spanish Armada, there was erected on Plymouth Hoe a monument with the inscription: "God sent his wind and they were scattered." When the people of England saw how the storm and the gale had shattered the Spanish Armada, they said: "God did it." When we are faced with any great and demanding task, God is the ally we must never leave out of the reckoning. That which to us alone is impossible is always possible with him.

(ii) The second story the writer to the Hebrews takes is that of Rahab. It is told in *Joshua* 2: 1–21 and finds its sequel in *Joshua* 6: 25. When Joshua sent out spies to spy out the situation in Jericho, they found a lodging in the house of Rahab, a harlot. She protected them and enabled them to make their escape; and in return, when Jericho was taken she and her family were saved from the general slaughter. It is extraordinary how Rahab became imprinted on the memory of Israel. *James* (2: 25) quotes her as a great example of the good works which demonstrate faith. The Rabbis were proud to trace their descent to her. And, amazingly, she is one of the names which appear in the genealogy of Jesus (*Matthew* 1: 5). Clement of Rome quotes her as an outstanding example of one who was saved "by faith and hospitality."

When the writer to the Hebrews cites her, the point he desires to make is this—Rahab in face of all the facts believed in the God of Israel. She said to the spies whom she welcomed and hid: "I know that the Lord has given you the land. . . . For the Lord your God, is he who is God in heaven above, and on earth beneath" (*Joshua* 2: 9–11). At the moment when she was speaking, there seemed not one chance in a million that the children of Israel could capture Jericho. These nomads from the desert had no artillery and no siege-engines. Yet Rahab believed—and staked her whole

future on the belief—that God would make the impossible
possible. When commonsense pronounced the situation
hopeless, she had the uncommon sense to see beyond the
situation. The real faith and the real courage are those
which can take God's side when it seems doomed to defeat.
As Faber had it:

> "Thrice blest is he to whom is given
>     The instinct that can tell
> That God is on the field when he
>     Is most invisible.
>
> For right is right, since God is God;
>     And right the day must win;
> To doubt would be disloyalty,
>     To falter would be sin."

The Christian believes in that no man who takes the side of God
can ever ultimately be on the losing side for, even if he
knows earth's defeats, there is a victory whose trophies
are in heaven.


## THE HEROES OF THE FAITH

*Hebrews* 11: 32–34

And what more shall I say? Time will fail me if I try to recount
the story of Gideon, of Barak, of Samson, of Jephthah, of David,
of Samuel and of the prophets, men who, through faith, mastered
kingdoms, did righteousness, obtained promises, shut the mouths
of lions, quenched the power of fire, escaped the edge of the
sword, from weakness were made strong, showed themselves
strong in warfare, routed the ranks of aliens.

IN this passage the writer lets his mind's eye roam back
over the history of his people; and out of it there springs to
memory name after name of those who were heroic souls.
He does not take them in any particular order but, as we
shall see when we look at the outstanding characteristics of
each  there is a line of thought which binds them all together.

The story of Gideon is told in *Judges* 6 and 7. With only three hundred men Gideon won a victory over the Ammonites in days when they had terrorized Israel, a victory which went ringing down the centuries. The story of Barak is in *Judges* 4 and 5. Under the inspiration of the prophetess Deborah, Barak assembled ten thousand young men and faced the fearful odds of the Canaanites with their nine hundred chariots of iron to win an almost incredible victory. It was as if a band of almost unarmed infantry had routed a division of tanks. The story of Samson is in *Judges* 13 to 16. Always Samson was fighting alone. In the isolation of his splendid strength again and again he faced the most amazing odds and emerged triumphant. He was the scourge of the Philistines. The story of Jephthah is in *Judges* 11 and 12. Jephthah was an illegitimate son; he was driven into a kind of exile and into the life of an outlaw; but when the Ammonites were putting Israel into fear, the forgotten outlaw was called back and won a tremendous victory, although his vow to God cost him the life of his daughter. There was David, who had once been a shepherd lad and who, to his own and everyone else's astonishment, was anointed king in preference to all his brothers (1 *Samuel* 16: 1–13). There was Samuel, born to his mother so late in life (1 *Samuel* 1), again and again moving alone as the only strong and faithful man of God amongst an easily frightened, discontented and rebellious people. There were the prophets, man after man of them bearing a faithful and isolated witness to God.

The whole list is of men who faced incredible odds for God. It is of men who never believed that God was on the side of the big battalions and were willing to take tremendous and even terrifying risks for him. It is of men who cheerfully and courageously and confidently accepted God-given tasks which, on human terms, were impossible. They were all men who were never afraid to stand alone and to face immense odds for the sake of their loyalty to God. The honour roll of history is of men who chose to be in God's minority rather than with earth's majority.

In the second part of the passage the writer to the Hebrews tells what these men did and others like them in a series of machine-gun-like phrases. For most of us much of their impact may be lost, for this reason—*phrase after phrase is a reminiscence*. For those who knew the scriptures well in their Greek version, phrase after phrase would ring a bell in the mind. The word used for *mastering kingdoms* is what Josephus, the Jewish historian, used of David. The phrase used for *wrought righteousness* is the description of David in 2 *Samuel* 8: 15. The expression used for *stopping the mouths of lions* is that used of Daniel in *Daniel* 6: 18, 23. The phrase about *quenching the violence of fire* goes straight back to the story of Shadrach, Meshach and Abed-nego in *Daniel* 3: 19–28. To speak about *escaping the edge of the sword* was to direct men's thoughts to the way in which Elijah escaped threatened assassination in 1 *Kings* 19: 1ff and Elisha in 2 *Kings* 6: 31ff. The trumpet call about being *strong in warfare* and *routing the ranks of the aliens* would immediately make men think of the unforgettable glories of the Maccabaean days.

The phrase about *being made strong out of weakness* might conjure up many a picture. It might paint the mental picture of the extraordinary healing of Hezekiah after he had turned his face to the wall to die (2 *Kings* 20: 1–7). Perhaps more likely in the time in which the writer to the Hebrews wrote, it would remind his hearers of that epic but bloodthirsty incident told in the *Book of Judith*, one of the apocryphal books. There was a time when Israel was threatened by the armies of Nebuchadnezzar led by his general Holofernes. The Jewish town of Bethulia had determined to surrender in five days' time for its supplies of food and water were at an end. In the town there was a widow called Judith. She was wealthy and beautiful but she had lived in lonely mourning since her husband Manasses had died. She dressed in all her finery, persuaded her people to let her out of the town and went straight to the camp of the Assyrians. She gained entry into the presence of Holofernes and persuaded him that she was convinced of the defeat of her people as a punishment

for their sins. She offered him a way into Jerusalem by
stealth; and then, having gained his confidence, she slew
him in his drunken sleep with his own dagger, cut off his head
and carried it back to her people. The traitors within the
camp were silenced and looming defeat was turned into
tumultuous victory. A woman's weakness had become strength
to save her country.

The writer to the Hebrews is here seeking to inspire new
courage and a new sense of responsibility by making his
hearers remember their past. He does not do it blatantly but
with infinite artistry. He does not so much tell them what to
remember as by delicate hints compel them to remember for
themselves. When Oliver Cromwell was arranging for the
education of his son Richard, he said: "I would have him
learn a little history." When we are discouraged, let us
remember and take heart again. God's arm is not shortened;
his power is not grown less. What he did once he can do
again, for the God of history is the same one as we worship
today.

## THE DEFIANCE OF SUFFERING

*Hebrews* 11: 35–40

Women received back their own folk as if they had been raised
from the dead. Others were crucified because they refused to
accept release, for they were eager to obtain a better resurrection.
Others went through scoffing and scourging, yes, and chains and
imprisonment. They were stoned; they were sawn asunder; they
underwent every kind of trial; they died by the murder of the
sword. They went about in sheepskins, in goatskins, they were in
want, they were oppressed, they were maltreated—the world was
not worthy of them—they wandered in desert places and on the
mountains, they lived in caves and in holes of the earth. All
these, though they were attested through their faith, did not receive
the promise, because God had some better plan for us, that they,
without us, should not find all his purposes fulfilled.

IN this passage the writer to the Hebrews is intermingling different periods of history. Sometimes he takes his illustrations from the Old Testament period; but still more he takes them from the Maccabaean period which falls between the Old and the New Testaments.

First let us take the things that can be explained against the Old Testament background. In the lives of Elijah (1 *Kings* 17: 17ff.) and of Elisha (2 *Kings* 4: 8ff.) we read how, by the power and the faith of the prophets, women did receive back again their children who had died. 2 *Chronicles* 24: 20–22 tells how the prophet Zechariah was stoned by his own people because he told them the truth. Legend had it that down in Egypt Jeremiah was stoned to death by his fellow-countrymen. Jewish legend tells that Isaiah was sawn asunder. Hezekiah, the good king, died; and Manasseh came to the throne. He worshipped idols and tried to compel Isaiah to take part in his idolatry and to approve of it. Isaiah refused and was condemned to be sawn asunder with a wooden saw. While his enemies tried to make him recant his faith he steadfastly defied them and prophesied their doom. "And whilst the saw cut into his flesh, Isaiah uttered no complaint and shed no tears; but he ceased not to commune with the Holy Spirit till the saw had cloven him to the middle of his body."

Even more the mind of the writer to the Hebrews goes back over the terrible days of the Maccabaean struggle. That is a struggle of which every Christian should know something, for if in these killing times, the Jews had surrendered their faith, Jesus could not have come. The story is like this.

About the year 170 B.C. there was on the throne of Syria a king called Antiochus Epiphanes. He was a good governor but he had an almost abnormal love for all things Greek and saw himself as a missionary for the Greek way of life. He tried to introduce this into Palestine. He had some success; there were those who were willing to accept Greek culture, Greek drama, Greek athletics. Greek athletes trained naked and some of the Jewish priests even went so far as to seek to obliterate the mark of circumcision from their bodies so that they might become completely hellenized. So far, Antiochus had succeeded only in causing a division in the nation; the greater part of the Jews were unshakeably true to their faith and could not be moved. Force and violence had not yet been used.

Then about 168 B.C. the matter came to boiling-point. Antiochus had an interest in Egypt. He amassed an army and invaded that country. To his deep humiliation the Romans ordered him home. They did not send an army to oppose him; such was the might of Rome that they did not need to. They sent a senator called Popilius Laena with a small and quite unarmed suite. Popilius and Antiochus met on the boundaries of Egypt. They talked; they both knew Rome and they had been friendly. Then, very gently, Popilius told Antiochus that Rome did not wish him to proceed with the campaign but wished him to go home. Antiochus said that he would consider it. Popilius took the staff which he was carrying and drew a circle in the sand round about Antiochus. Quietly he said: "Consider it now; you will give me your decision before you leave that circle." Antiochus thought for a moment and realized that to defy Rome was impossible. "I will go home," he said. It was a shattering humiliation for a king.

So Antiochus turned for home, almost mad with rage; and on the way he turned aside and attacked Jerusalem, capturing it almost without an effort. It was said that 80,000 Jews were killed and 10,000 sold into captivity. But there was worse to come. He sacked the Temple. The golden altars of the shewbread and of the incense, the golden candlestick, the golden vessels, even the curtains and the veils were taken. The treasury was sacked. Worse was to come. On the altar of the burnt offering he offered sacrifices of swine flesh to Zeus; and he turned the Temple chambers into brothels. No act of sacrilege was omitted. Still worse was to come. He completely forbade circumcision and the possession of the scriptures and of the law. He ordered the Jews to eat meats which were unclean and to sacrifice to the

Greek gods. Inspectors went throughout the land to see that these commands were carried out. And if any were found to defy them, they "underwent great miseries and bitter torments; for they were whipped with rods and their bodies were torn to pieces; they were crucified while they were still alive and breathed; they also strangled those women and their sons whom they had circumcised, as the king had appointed, hanging their sons about their necks as if they were upon their crosses. And if there were any sacred book of the law found, it was destroyed; and those with whom they were found miserably perished also" (Josephus, *Antiquities of the Jews,* 12: 5, 4). Never in all history has there been such a sadistic and deliberate attempt to wipe out a people's religion.

It is easy to see how this passage can be read against the terrible happenings of these days. The Book of Fourth Maccabees has two famous stories which were undoubtedly in the mind of the writer to the Hebrews when he made his list of the things that the man of faith has had to suffer.

The first is the story of Eleazar, the aged priest (4 *Maccabees* 5–7). He was brought before Antiochus and ordered to eat swine's flesh, being threatened with the direst penalties if he refused. He did refuse. "We, Antiochus," he said, "who are convinced that we live under a divine law, consider no compulsion to be so forcible as obedience to our law." He would not comply with the king's order, "no, not if you pluck out my eyes and consume my bowels in the fire." They stripped him naked and scourged him with whips, while a herald stood by him, saying: "Obey the king's commands," His flesh was torn off by the whips and he streamed down with blood and his flanks were laid open by wounds. He collapsed and one of the soldiers kicked him violently in the stomach to make him rise. In the end even the guards were moved to wondering compassion. They suggested to him that they would bring him dressed meat which was not pork, and that he should eat it pretending that it was pork. He refused. "We should thus ourselves become an example of impiety to the young, if we became to them an excuse for eating the unclean." In the end they carried him to the fire and threw him on it, "burning him with cruelly contrived instruments and pouring stinking liquids into his nostrils." So he died, declaring: "I am dying by fiery torments for the law's sake."

The second is the story of the seven brothers (4 *Maccabees* 8–14). They, too, were given the same choice and confronted with the same threats. They were confronted with "the wheels and racks and hooks and catapults and caldrons and frying pans and finger racks and iron hands and wedges and hot cinders." The first brother refused to eat the unclean things. They lashed him with whips and tied him to the wheel until he was dislocated and fractured in every limb. "They heaped up fuel and, setting fire to it, strained him upon the wheel still more. And the wheel was besmeared all over with blood, and the heap of coals was extinguished with the droppings of gore, and pieces of flesh flew about the axles of the machine." But he withstood their tortures and died faithful. The second brother they bound to the catapults. They donned spiked iron gloves. "These wild beasts, fierce as panthers, first dragged all the flesh off his sinews with their iron gauntlets to his chin and tore off the skin of his head." He, too, died faithful. The third brother was brought forward. "The officers, impatient at the man's boldness, dislocated his hands and feet with racking engines and wrenching them from their sockets, pulled his limbs asunder. And they fractured his fingers and his arms and his legs and his elbows." In the end they tore him apart on the catapult and flayed him alive. He, too, died faithful. They cut out the tongue of the fourth brother before they submitted him to like tortures. The fifth brother they bound to the wheel, bending his body round the edge of it, and then fastened him with iron fetters to the catapult and tore him in pieces. The sixth they broke upon the wheel "while a fire roasted him from beneath. Then they heated sharp spits and applied them to his back; and piercing through his sides they burned away his bowels." The seventh brother they roasted alive in a gigantic frying pan. These, too, died faithful.

These are the things of which the writer to the Hebrews is thinking; and these are things which we do well to remember. It was due to the faith of these men that the Jewish religion was not completely destroyed. If that religion had been destroyed, what would have happened to the purposes of God? How could Jesus have been born into the world if the Jewish religion had ceased to exist? In a very real way we owe our Christianity to these martyrs of the times when Antiochus made his deliberate attempt to wipe out the Jewish religion.

There came a day when the situation ignited. The agents of Antiochus had gone to a town called Modin and had erected an altar there to make the inhabitants do sacrifice to the Greek gods. The emissaries of Antiochus tried to persuade a certain Mattathias to set an example by offering sacrifice, for he was a distinguished and influential man. He refused in anger. But another Jew, seeking to curry favour and to save his own life, came forward and was about to sacrifice. Mattathias, moved to uncontrollable wrath, seized a sword and slew his apostate countryman and the king's commissioner with him.

The standard of rebellion was raised. Mattathias and his sons and those like-minded took to the hills; and once again the phrases used to describe their life there were in the mind of the writer to the Hebrews and he has echoes of them over and over again. "So Mattathias and his sons fled into the mountains, and left all that they ever had in the city" (1 *Maccabees* 2: 28). "Judas Maccabaeus (and his friends) withdrew himself into the wilderness and lived in the mountains, after the manner of beasts" (2 *Maccabees* 5: 27). "Others, who had run together into caves near by, to keep the Sabbath day secretly, being discovered . . . were all burnt together" (2 *Maccabees* 6: 11). "They wandered in the mountains and in the dens like beasts" (2 *Maccabees* 10: 6). In the end under Judas Maccabaeus and his brothers the Jews regained their freedom and the Temple was cleansed and the faith flourished again.

In this passage the writer to the Hebrews has done as before.

He does not actually mention these things. Far better that his hearers should be moved by this and that phrase to remember them for themselves.

In the end he says a great thing. All these died before the final unfolding of God's promise and the coming of his Messiah into the world. It was as if God had so arranged things that the full blaze of his glory should not be revealed until we and they can enjoy it together. The writer to the Hebrews is saying: "See! the glory of God has come. But see what it cost to enable it to come! That is the faith which gave you your religion. What can you do but be true to a heritage like that?"

## THE RACE AND THE GOAL

*Hebrews* 12: 1, 2

Therefore, since we have so great a cloud of witnesses enveloping us, let us strip off every weight and let us rid ourselves of the sin which so persistently surrounds us, and let us run with steadfast endurance the course that is marked out for us and, as we do so, let us keep our gaze fixed on Jesus who, in order to win the joy that was set before him, steadfastly endured the Cross, thinking nothing of its shame, and has now taken his seat at the right hand of the throne of God.

THIS is one of the great, moving passages of the New Testament; and in it the writer has given us a well-nigh perfect summary of the Christian life.

(i) In the Christian life we have *a goal*. The Christian is not an unconcerned stroller along the byways of life; he is a wayfarer on the high road. He is not a tourist, who returns each night to the place from which he starts; he is a pilgrim who is for ever on the way. The goal is nothing less than the likeness of Christ. The Christian life is going somewhere, and it would be well if, at each day's ending, we were to ask ourselves: "Am I any farther on?"

(ii) In the Christian life we have *an inspiration*. We have the thought of the unseen cloud of witnesses; and they are witnesses in a double sense, for they have witnessed their confession to Christ and they are now witnesses of our performance. The Christian is like a runner in some crowded stadium. As he presses on, the crowd looks down; and the crowd looking down are those who have already won the crown.

Longinus, in his great work *On The Sublime*, has a recipe for greatness in literary endeavour. "It is a good thing," he writes, "to form the question in our souls, 'How would Homer perhaps have said this? How would Plato or Demosthenes have lifted it up to sublimity? How would Thucydides have put it in his history?' For when the faces of these people come before us in our emulation, they will, as it were, illumine our road and will lift us up to those standards of perfection which we have imagined in our minds. It would be still better if we were to suggest this to our minds, 'What would this that I have said sound like to Homer, if he were standing by, or to Demosthenes, or how would they have reacted to it?' In truth it is a supreme test to imagine such a judgment court and theatre for our own private productions, and, in imagination, to submit an account of our writings to such heroes as judges."

An actor would act with double intensity if he knew that some famous dramatic master was sitting in the stalls watching him. An athlete would strive with double effort if he knew that a stadium of famous Olympic athletes was watching him. It is of the very essence of the Christian life that it is lived in the gaze of the heroes of the faith who lived, suffered and died in their day and generation. How can a man avoid the struggle for greatness with an audience like that looking down upon him?

(iii) In the Christian life we have *a handicap*. If we are encircled by the greatness of the past, we are also encircled by the handicap of our own sin. No man would seek to climb Mount Everest with a pantechnicon of lumber weighing him down. If we would travel far, we must travel light. There is in

life an essential duty of discarding things. There may be habits,
pleasures, self-indulgences, associations which hold us back.
We must shed them as the athlete sheds his track suit when
he goes to the starting-mark; and often we will need the help
of Christ to enable us to do so.

(iv) In the Christian life we have *a means*. That means is
*steadfast endurance*. The word is *hupomonē* which does not
mean the patience which sits down and accepts things but the
patience which masters them. It is not some romantic thing
which lends us wings to fly over the difficulties and the hard
places. It is a determination, unhurrying and yet undelaying,
which goes steadily on and refuses to be deflected. Obstacles
do not daunt it and discouragements do not take its hope away.
It is the steadfast endurance which carries on until in the end
it gets there.

(v) In the Christian life we have *an example*. That example
is Jesus himself. For the goal that was set before him, he
endured all things; to win it meant the way of the Cross. The
writer to the Hebrews has a flash of insight—*despising the
shame,* he says. Jesus was sensitive; never had any person so
sensitive a heart. A cross was a humiliating thing. It was for
criminals, for those whom society regarded as the dregs of
humanity—and yet he accepted it. St. Philip of Neri bids us
"to despise the world, to despise ourselves, and to despise the
fact that we are despised" (*spernere mundum, spernere te ipsum,
spernere te sperni*). If Jesus could endure like that, so must we.

(vi) In the Christian life we have *a presence,* the presence
of Jesus. He is at once the goal of our journey and the
companion of our way; at once the one whom we go to meet
and the one with whom we travel. The wonder of the Christian
life is that we press on surrounded by the saints, oblivious to
everything but the glory of the goal and for ever in the company
of him who has already made the journey and reached the goal,
and who waits to welcome us when we reach the end.

## THE STANDARD OF COMPARISON

*Hebrews 12: 3, 4*

> Consider him who steadfastly endured such opposition at the hands
> of sinners, and compare your lives with his, so that you may not
> faint and grow weary in your souls. You have not yet had to resist
> to the point of blood in your struggle against sin.

THE writer to the Hebrews uses two very vivid words when he
speaks of *fainting* and *growing weary*. They are the words
which Aristotle uses of an athlete who flings himself on the
ground in collapse *after* he has surged past the winning post
of the race. So Hebrews is in effect saying: "Don't give up too
soon; don't collapse until the winning post is passed.

To urge them to that he uses two arguments.

(i) For them the struggle of Christianity has not yet become
a mortal struggle. When he speaks of resisting to the point of
blood, he uses the very phrase of the Maccabaean leaders when
they called on their troops to fight to the death. When the
writer to the Hebrews says that his people have not yet resisted
to the point of blood, as Moffatt puts it, "he is not blaming
them, he is *shaming* them." When they think of what the heroes
of the past went through to make their faith possible, surely
they cannot drift into lethargy or flinch from conflict.

(ii) He pleads with them to compare what they have to suffer
with what Jesus suffered. He gave up the glory which was his;
he came into all the narrowness of the life of humanity; he
faced the hostility of men; in the end he had to die upon a
cross. So the writer to the Hebrews in effect demands: "How
can you compare what you have to go through with what he
went through? He did all that for you—what are you going to
do for him?"

These two verses stress the essential costliness of Christian
faith. It cost the lives of the martyrs; it cost the life of him
who was the Son of God. A thing which cost so much cannot
be lightly discarded. A heritage like that is not something that
a man can hand down tarnished. These two verses make the

demand that comes to every Christian: "Show yourself worthy of the sacrifice that men and God have made for you."

## THE DISCIPLINE OF GOD

*Hebrews* 12: 5–11

Have you forgotten the appeal, an appeal which reasons with you as sons?

"My son, do not treat lightly the discipline which the Lord sends;
Never lose heart when you are put to the test by him;
For the Lord disciplines the man whom he loves, and scourges every son whom he receives."

It is for the sake of discipline that you must endure. It is because he is treating us as sons that God sends these things upon us. What son is there whom his father does not discipline? If you are left without discipline—that discipline which everyone must share— then you are bastards and not sons. Surely it is true that we have human fathers who discipline us, and we pay heed to them. Surely we are still more bound to submit to the Father of the spirits of men, for that is the only way in which we can find real life. It was only for a short time that our human fathers disciplined us, and they did it as they thought best; but God disciplines us for our highest good and he does so to make us fit to share his own holiness. No discipline seems to be a thing of joy when we are actually undergoing it but afterwards it yields a fruit which is all to our highest welfare—the fruit of a righteous life—to those who are trained by it.

THE writer to the Hebrews sets out still another reason why men should cheerfully bear affliction when it comes to them. He has urged them to bear it because the great saints of the past have borne it. He has urged them to bear it because anything they may have to bear is a little thing compared with what Jesus Christ had to bear. Now he says that they must bear hardship because it is sent as a discipline from God and no life can have any value apart from discipline.

A father always disciplines his child. It would not be a mark of love to let a son do what he likes and have nothing but an easy way; it would show that the father regarded the son as no better than an illegitimate child to whom he felt neither love nor responsibility. We submit to an earthly father's discipline which is imposed only for a short time, until we reach years of maturity, and which at best always contains an element of arbitrariness. The earthly father is he to whom we owe our bodily life; how much more should we submit to the discipline of God to whom we owe our immortal spirits and who, in his wisdom, seeks for nothing but our highest good.

There is a curious passage in Xenophon's *Cyropaedia*. There is an argument about whether the man who makes men laugh or makes them weep is of most use in the world. Aglaitidas says: "He that makes his friends laugh seems to me to do them much less service than he who makes them weep; and if you will look at it rightly, you, too, will find that I speak the truth. At any rate, fathers develop self-control in their sons by making them weep and teachers impress good lessons on their pupils in the same way, and laws, too, turn the citizens to justice by making them weep. But could you say that those who make us laugh either do good to our bodies or make our minds any more fitted for the management of our private business or the affairs of state?" It was the view of Aglaitidas that it was the man who exerted discipline who really did good to his fellow-men.

There is no doubt that this passage would come to those who heard it for the first time with a double impact, for all the world knew of that amazing thing the *patria potestas,* the father's power. A Roman father had by law absolute power over his family. If his son should marry, the father continued to have absolute power both over him and any grandchildren there might be. It began at the beginning. A Roman father could keep or discard his newborn child as he liked. He could bind or scourge his son; he could sell him into slavery; and he even had the right to execute him. True, when a father was about to take serious steps against a member of his family, he usually

called a council of all its adult male members, but he did not
need to. True, later on public opinion would not permit the
execution of a son by a father, but it happened as late as the
time of Augustus. Sallust, the Roman historian, tells us of an
incident during the Catiline conspiracy. Catiline rebelled
against Rome and amongst those who went out to join his
forces was Aulus Fulvius, the son of a Roman senator. He was
arrested and brought back, and his own father tried him and
judged him and ordered him to be put to death. In regard to
the *patria potestas* a Roman son never came of age. He might
have engaged on a state career; he might be holding the highest
magistracies; he might be held in honour by the whole country;
all that did not matter; he was directly and completely under
his father's power so long as his father survived. If ever a people
knew what parental discipline was the Romans did; and when
the writer to the Hebrews talked about the way in which an
earthly father disciplined his son, his hearers well knew what
he was talking about.

So, then, the writer insists that we must look on all the
hardships of life as the discipline of God and as sent to work,
not for our harm but for our ultimate and highest good. To
prove his point he makes a quotation from *Proverbs* 3: 11, 12.
There are many ways in which a man may look at the discipline
which God sends him.

(i) He may resignedly *accept* it. That is what the Stoics did.
They held that nothing in this world happens outside the will
of God; therefore, they argued, there is nothing to do but to
accept it. To do anything else is simply to batter one's head
against the walls of the universe. That is possibly the acceptance of supreme wisdom; but none the less it is the
acceptance not of a father's love but of a father's power. It is
not a willing but a defeated acceptance.

(ii) A man may accept discipline *with the grim sense of getting
it over as soon as possible.* A certain famous Roman said: "I will
let nothing interrupt my life." If a man accepts discipline like
that he regards it as an infliction to be struggled through with
defiance and certainly not with gratitude.

(iii) A man may accept discipline *with the self-pity which leads in the end to collapse*. Some people, when they are caught up in some difficult situation, give the impression that they are the only people in the world whom life ever hurt. They are lost in their self-pity.

(iv) A man may accept discipline *as a punishment which he resents*. It is strange that at this time the Romans saw in national and personal disasters nothing but the vengeance of the gods. Lucan wrote: "Happy were Rome indeed, and blessed citizens would she have, if the gods were as much concerned with caring for men as they are with exacting vengeance from them." Tacitus held that the disasters of the nation were proof that not men's safety but men's punishment was the interest of the gods. There are still people who regard God as vindictive. When something happens to them or to those whom they love their question is: "What did I do to deserve this?" And the question is asked in such a tone as to make it clear that they regard the whole matter as an unjust punishment from God. It never dawns upon them to ask: "What is God trying to teach me and to do with me through this experience?"

(v) So we come to the last attitude. A man may accept discipline *as coming from a loving father*. Jerome said a paradoxical but true thing: "The greatest anger of all is when God is no longer angry with us when we sin." He meant that the supreme punishment is when God lets us alone as unteachable. The Christian knows that "a father's hand will never cause his child a needless tear" and that everything can be utilised to make him a wiser and a better man. As Robert Browning wrote in *Rabbi ben Ezra*:

> "Then welcome each rebuff
> That turns earth's smoothness rough,
> Each sting that bids nor sit nor stand but go!
> Be our joy three-parts pain!
> Strive and hold cheap the strain;
> Learn, nor account the pang; dare, never grudge the throe!

> For thence—a paradox
> Which comforts while it mocks—
> Shall life succeed in that it seems to fail;
> What I aspired to be,
> And was not, comforts me.
> A brute I might have been, but would not sink i' the scale."

We shall cease from self-pity, from resentment and from rebellious complaint if we remember that there is no discipline of God which does not take its source in love and is not aimed at good.

## DUTIES, AIMS AND DANGERS

*Hebrews* 12: 12–17

So, then, lift up the slack hands. Strengthen the weak knees. And make straight the paths of your feet so that the bones of the lame may not be completely dislocated but rather may be cured. Make peace your aim—and do it all together—and aim at that holiness without which no one can see the Lord. Watch that no one misses the grace of God. Watch that no pernicious influence grows up to involve you in troubles. And watch that the main body of your people are not soiled by any such thing. Watch that no one falls into sexual impurity or turns to an unhallowed life, as Esau did, Esau who, for a single meal, gave away his birthright. For you are well aware of how when he afterwards wanted to claim the blessing he ought to have inherited, he was rejected—for he had no opportunity to change his mind—although he sought that blessing with tears.

WITH this passage the writer to the Hebrews comes to the problems of everyday Christian life and living. He knew that sometimes it is given to a man to mount up with wings as an eagle; he knew that sometimes a man is enabled to run and not be weary in the pursuit of some great moment of endeavour; but he also knew that of all things it is hardest to walk every day and not to faint. Here he is thinking of the daily struggle of the Christian way.

(i) He begins by reminding them of their *duties*. In every congregation and in every Christian society there are those who are weaker and more likely to go astray and to abandon the struggle. It is the duty of those who are stronger to put fresh vigour into listless hands and fresh strength into failing feet. The phrase used for *slack hands* is the same as is used to describe the children of Israel in the days when they wished to abandon the rigours of the journey across the wilderness and to return to the ease and the fleshpots of Egypt.

*The Odes of Solomon* (6: 14ff.) have a description of the work of those who are true servants and ministers:

> "They have assuaged the dry lips,
> And the will that fainted they have raised up . . .
> And limbs that had fallen
> They have straightened and set up."

One of life's greatest glories is to be an encourager of the man who is near to despair and a strengthener of the man whose strength is failing. To help these people we have to make their ways straight. A Christian has a double duty; he has a duty to God and a duty to his fellow men. *The Testimony of Simeon* (5: 2, 3) has an illuminating description of the duty of the good man. "Make your heart good in the sight of the Lord; and make your ways straight in the sight of men; so you will find favour in the sight of the Lord and of men."

To God a man must present a clean heart; to men he must present an upright life. To show a man the right way to walk, by personal example to keep him on the right road, to remove from the path something that would make him stumble, to make the journey easier for faltering and lagging feet, is a Christian duty. A man must offer his heart to God and his service and example to his fellow-men.

(ii) The writer to the Hebrews turns to the *aims* which must ever be before the Christian.

(*a*) He must aim at *peace*. In Hebrew thought and language peace was no negative thing; it was intensely positive. It was not simply freedom from trouble; it was two things.

First, it was everything which makes for a man's highest good. As the Hebrews saw it, that highest good was to be found in obedience to God. *Proverbs* says: "My son, forget not my law; but let thine heart keep my commandments: for length of days and long life and *peace* shall they add unto thee." The Christian must aim at that complete obedience to God in which life finds its highest happiness, its greatest good, its perfect consummation, its *peace*. Second, *peace* meant right relationships between man and man. It meant a state when hatred was banished and each man sought nothing but his neighbour's good. Hebrews says: "Seek to live together as Christian men ought to live, in the real unity which comes from living in Christ."

The peace to be sought is that coming from obedience to God's will, which raises a man's life to its highest realization and enables him to live in and to produce right relationships between his fellow-men.

One thing remains to be noted—that kind of peace is to be *pursued*. It requires an effort; it is not something which just happens. It is the product of mental and spiritual toil and sweat. Rudyard Kipling wrote:

"Our England is a garden, and such gardens are not made
By singing:—'Oh, how beautiful!' and sitting in the shade,
While better men than we go out and start their working-lives
At grubbing weeds from gravel-paths with broken dinner-knives."

The gifts of God are given, but they are not given away; they have to be *won,* for they can be received only on God's conditions—and the supreme condition is obedience to himself.

(*b*) He must aim at *holiness* (*hagiasmos*). *Hagiasmos* has in it the same root as the adjective *hagios,* which is usually translated *holy*. The root meaning is always *difference* and *separation*. Although he lives in the world, the man who is *hagios* must always in one sense be different from it and separate from it. His standards are not the world's standards, nor his conduct the world's conduct. His aim is not to stand well with men but to stand well with God. *Hagiasmos,* as Westcott finely put it, is "the preparation for the presence of God." The life of the Christian is dominated by the constant memory that its greatest aim is to enter into the presence of God.

(iii) The writer to the Hebrews goes on to point the *dangers* which threaten the Christian life.

(*a*) There is the danger of *missing the grace of God.* The word he uses might be paraphrased *failing to keep up with the grace of God.* The early Greek commentator Theophylact interprets this in terms of a journey of a band of travellers who every now and again check up, "Has anyone fallen out? Has anyone been left behind while the others have pressed on?" In *Micah* there is a vivid text (4: 6), "I will assemble the lame." Moffatt translates it: "I will collect the stragglers." It is easy to straggle away, to linger behind, to drift instead of to march, and so to miss the grace of God. There is no opportunity in this life which cannot be missed. The grace of God brings to us the opportunity to make ourselves and to make life what they are meant to be. A man may, in his lethargy, his thoughtlessness, his unawareness, his procrastination, miss the chances which grace brings to him. Against that we must ever be upon the watch.

(*b*) There is the danger of what the Revised Standard Version calls "a root bearing poisonous and bitter fruit." The phrase comes from *Deuteronomy* 29: 18; and there it describes the man who goes after strange gods and encourages others to do so, and who thereby becomes a pernicious influence on the life of the community. The writer to the Hebrews is warning against those who are a corrupting influence. There are always those who think the Christian standards unnecessarily strict and punctilious; there are always those who do not see why they should not accept the world's standards of life and conduct. This was specially so in the early Church. It was a little island of Christianity surrounded by a sea of paganism; its members were, at the most, only one generation away from heathenism. It was easy to relapse into the old standards. This is a warning against the infection of the world, sometimes deliberately, sometimes unconsciously, spread within the Christian society.

(c) There is the danger of *falling into immorality or relapsing into an unhallowed life*. The word used for *unhallowed* is *bebēlos*. It has an illuminating background. It was used for ground that was *profane* in contradistinction to ground that was *consecrated*. The ancient world had its religions into which only the initiated could come. *Bebēlos* was used for the person who was *uninitiated* and *uninterested* in contradistinction to the man who was *devout*. It was applied to such men as Antiochus Epiphanes who was pledged to wipe out all true religion; it was applied to Jews who had become apostates and had forsaken God. Westcott sums up this word by saying that it describes the man whose mind recognizes nothing higher than earth, for whom there is nothing sacred, who has no reverence for the unseen. An *unhallowed* life is a life without any awareness of or interest in God. In its thoughts, aims, pleasures, it is completely earthbound. We have to have a care lest we drift into a frame of mind and heart which has no horizon beyond this world, for that way inevitably lie the failure of chastity and the loss of honour.

To sum it all up, the writer to the Hebrews cites the example of Esau. He really puts two stories together—*Genesis* 25: 28–34 and *Genesis* 27: 1–39. In the first Esau came in from the field ravenously hungry and sold his birthright to Jacob for a share of the food which he was preparing. The second story tells how Jacob subtly robbed Esau of his birthright by impersonating him when Isaac was old and blind and so gaining the blessing which belonged to Esau as the elder of the two sons. It was when Esau sought the blessing that Jacob had shrewdly obtained and learned he could not get it that he lifted up his voice and wept (*Genesis* 27: 38).

There is more to this than lies upon the surface. In Hebrew legend and in rabbinic elaboration Esau had come to be looked upon as the entirely sensual man, the man who put the needs of his body first. Hebrew legend says that while Jacob and Esau—they were twins—were still in their mother's womb,

Jacob said to Esau: "My brother, there are two worlds before us, this world and the world to come. In this world men eat and drink and traffic and marry and bring up sons and daughters; but all this does not take place in the world to come. If you like, take this world and I will take the other." And Esau was well content to take this world, because he did not believe that there was any other. On that very day when Jacob's subterfuge gained him Isaac's blessing, legend said that Esau already had committed five sins—"he had worshipped with strange worship, he had shed innocent blood, he had pursued a betrothed damsel, he had denied the life of the world to come, and he had despised his birthright."

Hebrew interpretation saw Esau as the sensual man, the man who saw no pleasures beyond the crude pleasures of this world. Any man like that sells his birthright; for a man throws away his inheritance when he throws away eternity.

The writer to the Hebrews says, according to the Authorized Version, that Esau *found no place for repentance.* The Greek for repentance is *metanoia,* which literally means *a change of mind.* It is better to say that it was now impossible for Esau to change his mind. It is not that he was barred from the forgiveness of God. It is just the grim fact that there are certain choices which cannot be unmade and certain consequences which not even God can take away. To take a very simple example—if a young man loses his purity or a girl her virginity, nothing can ever bring it back. The choice has been made and it stands. God can and will forgive but he cannot turn back the clock.

We do well to remember that there is a certain finality in life. If, like Esau, we take the way of this world and make bodily things our final good, if we choose the pleasures of time in preference to the joys of eternity, God can and will still forgive but something has happened that can never be undone. There are certain things in which a man cannot change his mind but must abide for ever by the choice that he has made.

## THE TERROR OF THE OLD AND THE GLORY OF THE NEW

*Hebrews* 12: 18–24

It is not to something that can be touched that you have come, to a flaming fire, to mist and gloom and stormblast, and to the blare of a trumpet, and to a voice which spoke such words that those who heard it begged that not another word should be further spoken unto them, for they could not bear the command: "If even a beast touches the mountain, it shall be stoned." So terrifying was the apparition that Moses said: "I am in utter fear and trembling." But you have come to Mount Sion and to the city of the living God, the heavenly Jerusalem, to ten thousands of angels gathered in glad assembly, to the assembly of the honoured ones whose names are in the registers of heaven, to that God who is judge of all, to the spirits of just men who have come to that goal for which they were created, and to Jesus, the mediator of the new covenant, to the sprinkled blood which has a message greater than the blood of Abel.

THIS passage is a contrast between the old and the new. It is a contrast between the giving of the law on Mount Sinai and the new covenant of which Jesus is the mediator. Down to verse 21 it has echo after echo of the story of the giving of the law on Mount Sinai. *Deuteronomy* 4: 11 describes that first lawgiving: "And you came near and stood at the foot of the mountain; while the mountain burned with fire to the heart of heaven, wrapped in darkness, cloud and gloom. And the Lord spoke to you out of the midst of the fire." *Exodus* 19: 12, 13 tells of the unapproachability of that awful mountain: "And you shall set bounds for the people round about, saying, 'Take heed that you do not go up into the mountain, or touch the border of it: whoever touches the mountain shall be put to death: no hand shall touch him, but he shall be stoned, or shot; whether beast or man, he shall not live: When the trumpet sounds a long blast they shall come up to the mountain.'" *Deuteronomy* 5: 23–27 tells how the people were so afraid to hear the voice of God for themselves that they asked Moses to go and to bring God's message to them. "If we hear the voice of the Lord our God any more, we shall die."

*Deuteronomy* 9: 19 tells of the terror of Moses, but the writer to the Hebrews has transferred these words to the giving of the law, although in the original story they were spoken by Moses when he came down from the mountain and found the people worshipping the golden calf. The whole passage down to verse 21 is a pattern of reminiscences from the story of the giving of the law at Mount Sinai. All the terrifying things have been gathered together to stress the awfulness of that scene.

In the giving of the law at Mount Sinai three things are stressed. (i) *The sheer majesty of God.* The story stresses the shattering might of God and in it there is no love at all. (ii) *The absolute unapproachability of God.* So far from the way being open to God, he who tries to approach him meets death. (iii) *The sheer terror of God.* Here is nothing but an awe-stricken fear which is afraid to look and even to listen.

Then at verse 22 comes the difference. The first section deals with all that man can expect under the old covenant, a God of lonely majesty, complete separation from man, and prostrating fear. But to the Christian there has come the new covenant and a new relationship with God.

Hebrews makes a kind of list of the new glories that await the Christian.

(i) The new Jerusalem awaits him. This world with all its impermanence, its fears, its mysteries, its separations goes and life for the Christian is made new.

(ii) The angels await him in joyful assembly. The word used for *joyful assembly* is *panēguris* which is the word for a joyful national assembly in honour of the gods. To the Greek it described a joyful holy day when all men rejoiced. For the Christian, the joy of heaven is such that it makes even the angels break into rejoicing.

(iii) There await him God's elected people. The writer to the Hebrews uses two words to describe them. He says literally that they are *the first-born*. Now the characteristic of the *first-born* son is that the inheritance and the honour are his. He says that they are those whose *names are written in the registers of heaven*. In ancient days kings kept a register of their faithful citizens. So there await the Christian all those whom God has honoured and all those whom God has reckoned amongst his faithful citizens.

(iv) There awaits him God the Judge. The writer to the Hebrews never forgot that, at the end, the Christian must stand the scrutiny of God. The glory is there; but the awe and the fear of God still remain. The New Testament is never in the slightest danger of sentimentalising the idea of God.

(v) There await him the spirits of all good men who have achieved their goal. Once they encircled him in the unseen cloud; now he will be one of them. He himself goes to join those whose names are on God's honour roll.

(vi) Finally the writer to the Hebrews says that it was Jesus who initiated this new covenant and made this new relationship with God possible. It was he, the perfect priest and the perfect sacrifice, who made the unapproachable approachable and he did this at the cost of his blood. So the section ends with a curious contrast between the blood of Abel and the blood of Jesus. When Abel was slain, his blood upon the ground called for vengeance (*Genesis* 4: 10); but when Jesus was slain, his blood opened up the way of reconciliation. His sacrifice made it possible for man to be friends with God.

Once men were under the terror of the law; the relationship between them and God was one of unbridgeable distance and shuddering fear. But after Jesus came and lived and died, the God who was far distant was brought near and the way opened to his presence.

## THE GREATER OBLIGATION

*Hebrews* 12: 25–29

See that you do not refuse to listen to his voice; for if they who refused to listen to the one who brought the oracles of God upon earth did not escape, how much more shall we not escape if we turn away from him who speaks from Heaven? Then his voice shook the earth but now the voice of the promise is: "Still once more I will shake not only the earth but heaven also." That phrase "still once more" signifies the removal of the things that are shaken, because they are merely created things, in order that the things which cannot be shaken may remain. Therefore let us give thanks because we are receiving a kingdom that cannot be shaken, a kingdom in which we must worship God acceptably, with reverence and with fear, for our God, too, is a consuming fire.

HERE the writer begins with a contrast which is also a warning. Moses brought to earth the oracles of God. The word that he uses (*chrēmatizein*) implies that Moses was only the *transmitter* of these oracles, the mouthpiece through which God spoke; and yet the man who broke these commandments did not escape punishment. On the other hand there is Jesus. The word used of him (*lalein*) implies the direct speech of God. He was not merely the transmitter of God's voice, he *was* God's voice. If that be so, how much more will the man who refuses to obey him find punishment? If a man merits condemnation for neglecting the imperfect message of the law, how much more does he merit it for neglecting the perfect message of the gospel? Because the gospel is the full revelation of God, there is laid on the man who hears it a double and a terrible responsibility; and his condemnation must be all the more if he neglects it.

Hebrews goes on to draw out another thought. When the law was given, the earth was shaken. "And Mount Sinai was wrapped in smoke, because the Lord descended upon it in fire; and the smoke of it went up like the smoke of a kiln, and the whole mountain quaked greatly" (*Exodus* 19: 18). "Tremble, O earth at the presence of the Lord" (*Psalm* 114: 7). "The earth quaked, the heavens poured down rain at the presence of God" (*Psalm* 68: 8). "The crash of thy thunder was in the whirlwind; thy lightnings lighted up the world; the earth trembled and shook" (*Psalm* 77: 18).

The writer to the Hebrews finds another reference to the shaking of the earth in *Haggai* 2: 6. There the Greek version of the Old Testament says: "Once again, in a little while, (the Hebrew says, "very soon") I will shake the heavens and the earth and the sea and the dry land." The writer to the Hebrews

takes this to be an announcement of the day when this earth
shall pass away and the new age will begin. In that day
everything that can be shaken will be destroyed; the only things
to remain will be the things which can never be shaken; and
chief among them is our relationship with God.

All things may pass away; the world as we know it may be
uprooted; life as we experience it may come to an end; but
one thing stands eternally sure—the relationship of the
Christian to God.

If that be so there is a great obligation laid upon us. We
must worship God with reverence and serve him with fear; for
nothing must be allowed to disturb that relationship which will
be our salvation when the world passes away. So the writer
to the Hebrews finishes with one of those threatening
quotations which he so often flings like a thunderbolt at his
readers. It is a quotation from *Deuteronomy* 4: 24. Moses is
telling the people that they must never break their agreement
with God and relapse into idolatry. For he is a jealous God.
They must worship him alone or they will find him a consuming
fire. It is as if the writer to the Hebrews was saying: "There
is a choice before you. Remain steadfastly true to God, and in
the day when the universe is shaken into destruction your
relationship with him will stand safe and secure. Be false to
him and that very God who might have been your salvation
will be to you a consuming fire of destruction." It is a grim
thought; but in it there is the eternal truth that, if a man is
true to God, he gains everything and, if he is untrue to God,
he loses everything. In time and in eternity nothing really
matters save loyalty to God.

## THE MARKS OF THE CHRISTIAN LIFE

*Hebrews* 13: 1–6

Let brotherly love be always with you.

Do not forget the duty of hospitality for, in remembering this
duty, there are some who have entertained angels without knowing
that they were doing so.

Remember those who are in prison for you yourselves know what it is like to be a prisoner; remember those who are suffering ill-treatment for the same thing can happen to you so long as you are in the body.

Let marriage be held in honour among you all and never let the marriage bed be defiled. God judges those who are adulterers and immoral in their conduct.

Let your way of life be free from the love of money. Be content with what you have for he has said: "I will never fail you and I will never forsake you"; so that we can say with confidence: "The Lord is my helper: I will not be afraid. What can man do to me?"

As he comes to the close of the letter, the writer to the Hebrews turns to practical things. Here he outlines five essential qualities of the Christian life.

(i) There is *brotherly love*. The very circumstances of the early Church sometimes threatened brotherly love. The very fact that they took their religion as seriously as they did was in one sense a danger. In a Church which is threatened from the outside and desperately in earnest in the inside, there are always two dangers. First, there is the danger of heresy-hunting. The very desire to keep the faith pure tends to make men eager to track down and eliminate the heretic and the man whose faith has gone astray. Second, there is the danger of stern and unsympathetic treatment of the man whose nerve and faith have failed. The very necessity of unswerving loyalty in the midst of a heathen and a hostile world tends to add rigourousness to the treatment of the man who in some crisis had not the courage to stand for his faith. It is a great thing to keep the faith clean; but when the desire to do so makes us censorious, harsh and unsympathetic, brotherly love is destroyed and we are left with a situation which may be worse than the one we tried to avoid. Somehow or other we have to combine two things—an earnestness in the faith and a kindness to the man who has strayed from it.

(ii) There is *hospitality*. The ancient world loved and honoured hospitality. The Jews had a saying: "There are six things the fruit of which a man eats in this world and by which his horn is raised in the world to come." And the list begins: "Hospitality to the stranger and visiting the sick." The Greeks gave Zeus, as one of his favourite titles, the title *Zeus Xenios,* which means Zeus, the god of strangers. The wayfaring man and the stranger were under the protection of the king of the gods. Hospitality, as Moffatt says, was an article of ancient religion.

Inns were filthy, ruinously expensive, and of low repute. The Greek had always a shrinking from hospitality given for money; inn-keeping seemed to him an unnatural affair. In *The Frogs* of Aristophanes, Dionysus asks Heracles, when they are discussing finding a lodging, if he knows where there are fewest fleas. Plato in *The Laws* speaks of the inn-keeper holding travellers to ransom. It is not without significance that Josephus says that Rahab, the harlot who harboured Joshua's scouts in Jericho, kept an inn. When Theophrastus wrote his character sketch of the reckless man, he said that he was fit to keep an inn or run a brothel; he put both occupations on the same level.

In the ancient world there was a rather wonderful system of what were called "guest friendships." Throughout the years families, even when they had lost active touch with each other, had an arrangement that at any time needful they would make accommodation available for each other. This hospitality was even more necessary in the circle of the Christians. Slaves had no home of their own to which to go. Wandering preachers and prophets were always on the roads. On the ordinary business of life, Christians had journeys to make. Both their price and their moral atmosphere made the public inns impossible. There must in those days have been many isolated Christians fighting a lonely battle. Christianity was, and still should be, the religion of the open door. The writer to the Hebrews says that those who have given hospitality to strangers have sometimes, all unaware, entertained the angels of God. He is thinking of the time when the angel came to Abraham and Sarah to tell them

of the coming of a son (*Genesis* 18: 1ff.) and of the day when
the angel came to Manoah to tell him that he would have
a son (*Judges* 13: 3ff.).

(iii) There is *sympathy for those in trouble*. It is here we
see the early Christian Church at its loveliest. It often
happened that the Christian landed in prison and worse. It
might be for his faith; it might be for debt, for the Christians
were poor; it might be that they were captured by pirates or
brigands. It was then that the Church went into action.

Tertullian in *The Apology* writes: "If there happen to be
any in the mines, or banished to the islands, or shut up in
prisons for nothing but their fidelity to the cause of God's
Church, they become the nurslings of their confession."
Aristides the heathen orator said of the Christians: "If they
hear that any one of their number is imprisoned or in distress
for the sake of their Christ's name, they all render aid in
his necessity and, if he can be redeemed, they set him free."
When Origen was young it was said of him: "Not only was
he at the side of the holy martyrs in their imprisonment and
until their final condemnation but, when they were led to
death, he boldly accompanied them into danger."

Sometimes Christians were condemned to the mines
which was almost like being sent to Siberia. *The Apostolic
Constitutions* lay it down: "If any Christian is condemned
for Christ's sake to the mines by the ungodly, do not
overlook him but from the proceeds of your toil and sweat
send him something to support himself and to reward the
soldier of Christ." The Christians sought out their fellow
Christians even in the wilds. There was actually a little
Christian Church in the mines at Phaeno.

Sometimes Christians had to be ransomed from robbers
and brigands. *The Apostolic Constitutions* lay it down: "All
monies accruing from honest labour do ye appoint and
apportion to the redeeming of the saints ransoming thereby
slaves and captives and prisoners, people who are sore abused
or condemned by tyrants." When the Numidian robbers
carried off their Christian friends, the Church at Carthage

raised the equivalent of £1,000 to ransom them and promised more. There were actually cases where Christians sold themselves as slaves to find money to ransom their friends.

They were even prepared to bribe their way into gaol. The Christians became so notorious for their help to those in gaol that at the beginning of the fourth century the Emperor Licinius passed new legislation that "no one was to show kindness to sufferers in prison by supplying them with food and that no one was to show mercy to those starving in prison." It was added that those who were discovered so doing would be compelled to suffer the same fate as those they tried to help.

These instances are taken from Harnack's *Expansion of Christianity* and many others could be added. In the early days no Christian in trouble for his faith was ever neglected or forgotten by his fellow Christians.

(iv) There is *purity*. First, the marriage bond is to be universally respected. This may mean either of two almost opposite things. (*a*) There were ascetics who despised marriage. Some even went the length of castrating themselves to secure what they thought was purity. Origen, for instance, took that course. Even a heathen like Galen, the physician, noted of the Christians that "they include men and women who refrain from cohabiting all their lives." The writer to the Hebrews insists against these ascetics that the marriage bond is to be honoured and not despised. (*b*) There were those who were ever liable to relapse into immorality. The writer to the Hebrews uses two words. The one denotes adulterous living; the other denotes all kinds of impurity, such as unnatural vice. Into the world the Christians brought a new ideal of purity. Even the heathen admitted that. Galen, in the passage we have already quoted, goes on: "And they also number individuals who, in ruling and controlling themselves and in their keen pursuit of virtue, have attained a pitch not inferior to that of real philosophers." When Pliny, the governor of Bithynia, examined the Christians and reported back to Trajan, the Emperor, he had to admit, even although he was looking for a charge on which to condemn them, that at their Lord's Day meeting: "They bound themselves by an oath not for any criminal end but to avoid theft or robbery or adultery, never to break their word nor repudiate a deposit when called upon to refund it." In the early days the Christians presented such a purity to the world that not even their critics and their enemies could find a fault in it.

(v) There is *contentment*. The Christians must be free from the love of money. He must be content with what he has, and why should he not be for he possesses the continual presence of God? Hebrews quotes two great Old Testament passages— *Joshua* 1: 5 and *Psalm* 118: 6—to show that the man of God needs nothing more because he has with him always the presence and the help of God. Nothing that man can give him can improve on that.

## THE LEADERS AND THE LEADER

*Hebrews* 13: 7, 8

> Remember your leaders, the men who spoke the word of God to you. Look back on how they made their exit from this life and imitate their faith. Jesus Christ is the same yesterday and today and for ever.

IMPLICIT in this passage is a description of the real leader of men.

(i) The real leader of the Church preaches Christ and thereby brings men to him. Leslie Weatherhead somewhere tells of a public schoolboy who decided to enter the ministry. He was asked when he had come to that decision and said it was after hearing a certain sermon in his school chapel. He was asked the name of the preacher and his answer was that he had no memory of the preacher's name. All he knew was that he had shown him Jesus. The duty of the real preacher is to obliterate himself and show men nothing but Christ.

(ii) The real leader of the Church lives in the faith and thereby brings Christ to men. A saint has been defined as "a man in whom Christ lives again." The duty of the real preacher is not so much to talk to men about Christ as to show them Christ in his own life. Men listen not so much to what he is saying as to what he is.

(iii) The real leader, if need be, dies in loyalty. He shows men how to live and is prepared to show them how to die. Jesus, having loved his own, loved them to the end; and the real leader, having loved Jesus, loves him to the end. His loyalty never stops halfway.

(iv) Thereby the real leader leaves to those who come after two things—an example and an inspiration. Quintilian, the Roman master of oratory, said: "It is a good thing to know, and always to keep turning over in the mind, the things which were illustriously done of old." Epicurus advised his disciples continuously to remember those of old time who lived with virtue.

If there is one thing more than another that the world and the Church need in every generation, it is leadership like that.

Then the writer to the Hebrews moves on to another great thought. It is in the nature of things that all earthly leaders must come and go. They have their part in the drama of life and then the curtain comes down. But Jesus Christ is the same yesterday and today and for ever. His pre-eminence is permanent; his leadership is for ever. Therein lies the secret of earthly leadership; the real leader is the man who is himself led by Jesus Christ. He who walked the ways of Galilee is as powerful as ever to smite evil and to love the sinner; and, as then he chose twelve to be with him and sent them out to do his work, so now he is still seeking those who will bring men to him and him to men.

## THE WRONG AND THE RIGHT SACRIFICE

*Hebrews* 13: 9–16

Do not let yourselves be carried away by subtle and strange teachings, for it is a fine thing to have your heart made strong by grace not by the eating of different kinds of food, for they never did any good to those who took that line of conduct. We have

an altar from which those who serve in the tabernacle have no
right to eat. For the bodies of the animals, whose blood is taken
by the High Priest into the Holy Place as an offering for sin, are
burned outside the camp. That was why Jesus suffered outside the
gate, so that he might make men fit for the presence of God by his
own blood. So then let us go to him outside the camp, bearing
the same reproach as he did, for here we have no abiding city
but are searching for the city which is to come. Through him,
therefore, let us continually bring to God a sacrifice of praise, I
mean, the fruit of lips which continually acknowledge their faith
in his name. Do not forget to do good and to share everything,
for God is well pleased with a sacrifice like that.

IT may be that no one will ever discover the precise meaning
behind this passage. Clearly there was some false teaching
going on in the Church to which this letter was written.
The writer to the Hebrews did not need to describe it; his
readers knew all about it, because some of them had succumbed
to it and all were in danger of it. As to what it was, we can
only guess.

We may start with one basic fact. The writer to the Hebrews
is convinced that real strength comes to a man's heart only
from the grace of God and that what people eat and drink
has nothing to do with their spiritual strength. So then in the
Church to which he was writing there were some who placed
too much importance on laws about food. There are certain
possibilities.

(i) The Jews had rigid food laws, laid down at length in
*Leviticus* 11. They believed they could serve and please God
by eating and by not eating certain foods. Possibly there
were some in this Church who were ready to abandon their
Christian liberty and once again put themselves under the
yoke of Jewish rules and regulations about food, thinking that
by so doing they were going to add strength to their spiritual
life.

(ii) Certain Greeks had very definite ideas about food. Long
ago Pythagoras had been like that. He believed in reincarnation,
that a man's soul passed from body to body until finally it

merited release. That release could be hastened by prayer and meditation and discipline and asceticism; and so the Pythagoreans were vegetarians. There were people called Gnostics who were much the same. They believed that matter was altogether bad and that a man must concentrate on spirit which is altogether good. They therefore believed that the body was altogether bad and that a man ought to discipline it and treat it with the greatest austerity. They cut down food to the bare minimum and they, too, abstained from meat. There were any number of Greeks who thought that by what they ate or refused to eat they were strengthening their spiritual life and releasing their soul.

(iii) Neither of these things seems quite to fit. This eating and drinking has something to do with the body of Jesus. The writer to the Hebrews goes back to the regulations for the Day of Atonement. According to these regulations, the body of the bullock which was an offering for the sins of the High Priest and the body of the goat which was an offering for the sins of the people must be totally consumed with fire in a place outside the camp (*Leviticus* 16: 27). They were sin offerings and the point is that even if the worshippers had wished to eat their flesh they could not do so. The writer to the Hebrews sees Jesus as the perfect sacrifice. The parallel for him is complete because Jesus, too, was sacrificed "outside the gate" that is, outside the city wall of Jerusalem. Crucifixions were always carried out outside a town. Jesus, then, was a sin-offering for men; and it follows that, just as none could eat of the flesh of the sin-offering on the Day of Atonement, no one can eat of his flesh.

It may be that here we have the clue. There may have been a little group in this Church who, either at the sacrament or at some common meal where they consecrated their food to Jesus, claimed that they were in fact eating the body of Christ. They may have persuaded themselves that because they had consecrated their food to Christ, his body had entered into it. That was indeed what the religious Greeks believed about their gods. When a Greek sacrificed he was given back part of the meat. Often he made a feast for himself and his friends within the temple where the sacrifice had been made; and he believed that when he ate the meat of the sacrifice, the god to whom that meat had been sacrificed was in it and entered into him. It may well be that certain Greeks had brought their own ideas into Christianity with them; and talked about eating the body of Christ.

The writer to the Hebrews believed with all the intensity of his being that no food can bring Christ into a man and that Christ can enter into him only by grace. It is quite likely that we have here a reaction against an overstressing of the sacraments. It is a notable fact that the writer to the Hebrews never mentions the sacraments; they do not seem to come into his scheme at all. It is likely that, even thus early, there were those who took a mechanical view of the sacraments, forgetting that no sacrament in the world avails anything by itself and that its only use is that in it the grace of God meets the faith of man. It is not the meat but the faith and the grace which matter.

This queer argument has set the writer to the Hebrews thinking. Christ was crucified outside the gate. He was exiled from men and numbered with the transgressors. Therein the writer to the Hebrews sees a picture. We, too, have to sever ourselves from the life of the world and be willing to bear the same reproach as Christ bore. The isolation and the humiliation may come to the Christian as they came to his Saviour.

Hebrews goes further. If the Christian cannot again offer the sacrifice of Christ, what can he offer? The writer says he can offer certain things.

(i) He can offer his continual praise and thanks to God. The ancient peoples sometimes argued that a thank-offering was more acceptable to God than a sin-offering, for when a man offered a sin-offering he was trying to get something for himself, while a thank-offering was the unconditional offering of the grateful heart. The sacrifice of gratitude is one that all may and should bring.

(ii) He can offer his public and glad confession of his faith in the name of Christ. That is the offering of loyalty. The Christian can always offer to God a life that is never ashamed to show whose it is and whom it serves.

(iii) The Christian can offer deeds of kindness to his fellow men. In fact that was something which a Jew knew well. After A.D. 70 the sacrifices of the Temple came to an end when the Temple was destroyed. The Rabbis taught that with the Temple ritual gone, theology, prayer, penitence, the study of the law and charity were sacrifices equivalent to the ancient ritual. Rabbi Jochanan ben Zakkai comforted himself in those sorrowful days by believing that "in the practice of charity he still possessed a valid sacrifice for sin." An ancient Christian writer says: "I expected that thy heart would bear fruit and that thou wouldst worship God, the Creator of all, and unto him continually offer thy prayers by means of compassion; for compassion shown to men by men is a bloodless sacrifice and holy unto God." After all, Jesus himself said: "As you did it to one of the least of these my brethren, you did it to me" (*Matthew* 25: 40). The best of all sacrifices to bring to God is the gift of help to one of his children in need.

## OBEDIENCE AND PRAYER

*Hebrews* 13: 17–20

Obey your leaders and submit to them, for they sleeplessly watch over your souls, conscious that they will have to give account of their trust. This do that they may carry out this task with joy and not with grief, for, if you grieve them, there would be no profit to you either in that. Keep on praying for us, for we believe that we have a clear conscience, for we wish in all things to live in such a way that our conduct will be fair. I urge you to do this all the more that I may the more quickly be enabled to return to you.

THE writer to the Hebrews lays down the duty of the congregation to its present leaders and its absent leader.

To the present leaders the duty of the congregation is obedience. A Church is a democracy but not a democracy run mad; it must give obedience to those whom it has chosen as its guides. That obedience is not to be given in order to gratify the leaders' sense of power or to increase their prestige. It is to be given so that at the end of the day the leaders may be seen to have lost none of the souls committed to their care. The greatest joy of the leader of any Christian fellowship is to see those whom he leads established in the Christian way. As John wrote: "No greater joy can I have than this, to hear that my children follow the truth" (3 *John* 4). The greatest sorrow of the leader of any Christian fellowship is to see those whom he leads growing further away from God.

To the absent leader the duty of the congregation is that of prayer. It is a Christian duty always to bear our absent loved ones to the throne of God's grace and daily to remember there all who bear the responsibility of leadership and authority. When Stanley Baldwin became Prime Minister of Great Britain, his friends thronged round to congratulate him. He said: "It is not your congratulations I need; it is your prayers."

We must give our respect and our obedience to those set in authority over us in the Church when they are present with us, and when they are absent we must remember them in our prayers.

## A PRAYER, A GREETING AND A BLESSING

*Hebrews* 13: 20–24

May the God of peace, who brought up from among the dead the great shepherd of the sheep with the blood of the eternal covenant, it is our Lord Jesus I mean, equip you with every good thing that you may do his will and may he create in you through Jesus Christ that which is well-pleasing in his sight. To him be glory for ever and ever. Amen.

Brothers, I appeal to you to bear with this appeal of mine, for indeed it is but a short letter that I have sent to you.

I would have you know that our brother Timothy is at liberty again. If he comes soon I will see you along with him.

Greet all your leaders and all God's dedicated people. The folk from Italy send you their greetings. Grace be with you all. Amen.

THE great prayer of the first two verses of this passage draws a perfect picture of God and of Jesus.

(i) God is the God of peace. Even in the most troublous and distressing situation, he can bring peace to men's souls. In any fellowship where there is division, it is because men have forgotten God and only the remembrance of his presence can bring back the lost peace. When a man's mind and heart are distracted and he is torn in two between the two sides of his own nature, it is only by giving his life into the control of God that he can know peace. It is only the God of peace who can make us at peace with ourselves, at peace with each other and at peace with himself.

(ii) God is the God of life. It was God who brought Jesus again from the dead. His love and power are the only things which can bring a man peace in life and triumph in death. It was to obey the will of God that Jesus died and that same will brought him again from the dead. For the man who obeys the will of God there is no such thing as final disaster; even death itself is conquered.

(iii) God is the God who both shows us his will and equips us to do it. He never gives us a task without also giving us the power to accomplish it. When God sends us out, he sends us equipped with everything we need.

The picture of Jesus is also threefold.

(i) Jesus is the great shepherd of his sheep. The picture of Jesus as the good shepherd is very precious to us but, strangely enough, it is one that Paul never uses and that the writer to the Hebrews uses only here. There is a lovely legend of Moses which tells of a thing he did when he had fled from Egypt and was keeping the flocks of Jethro in the desert. A sheep of the flock wandered far away. Moses patiently followed it and found it drinking at a mountain stream. He came up to it and put it upon his shoulder. "So it was because you were thirsty that you wandered away," said Moses gently and, without any anger at the toil the sheep had caused him, he carried it home. When God saw it, he said: "If Moses is so compassionate to a straying sheep, he is the very man I want to be the leader of my people." A shepherd is one who is ready to give his life for his sheep; he bears with their foolishness and never stops loving them. That is what Jesus does for us.

(ii) Jesus is the one who established the new covenant and made possible the new relationship between God and man. It was he who took away the terror and showed us the love of God.

(iii) Jesus is the one who died. To show men what God was like and to open the way to him, cost the life of Jesus. Our new relationship to God cost his blood.

The letter finishes with some personal greetings. The writer to the Hebrews half apologises for its length. If he had dealt with these vast topics the letter would never have ended at all. It is short—Moffatt points out that you can read it aloud in less than an hour—in comparison with the greatness of the eternal truths with which it deals.

What the reference to Timothy means no one knows, but it sounds as if he, too, had been in prison for the sake of Jesus Christ.

And so the letter closes with a blessing. All through it has been telling of the grace of Christ which opens the way to God and it comes to an end with a prayer that that wondrous grace may rest upon its readers.

# FURTHER READING

J. Moffatt, *Hebrews* (ICC; *G*)
W. Neil, *Hebrews* (Tch: *E*)
J. H. Robinson, *Hebrews* (MC; *E*)

## *Abbreviations*

ICC: International Critical Commentary
MC : Moffatt Commentary
Tch : Torch Commentary

*E* : English Text
*G* : Greek Text